D0916193

THE RISE OF THE AGILE LEADER

CAN YOU MAKE THE SHIFT?

CHUCK MOLLOR

Prominence Publishing
www.prominencepublishing.com

The Rise of the Agile Leader/Chuck Mollor. – 2nd ed.
ISBN: 978-1988925592

Table of Contents

What Leaders Are Saying About "The Rise of the Agile Leader"

"This is not your typical theory-based leadership book. Chuck Mollor artfully couples his framework with specific tactics and provides a blueprint for what organizations need to do to develop their current and future leaders. This actionable approach empowers the reader to put the principles of agile leadership into practice now. Mollor's decades of experience add a tried and true human element to the subject matter, making this an entertaining and highly valuable read."

Peter P. Dhillon

Chairman of the Board, Ocean Spray Cranberries

"Chuck Mollor cuts to the heart of key pitfalls and opportunities in leadership today. Reading The Rise of the Agile Leader is like having your own executive coach in the room. You can't help but recognize yourself in the examples he gives from his many years in management and coaching. His advice is concrete and actionable."

Deniz Razon

Chief Commercial Officer, Servier Pharmaceuticals

"Chuck Mollor's agile leadership framework perfectly captures what all leaders and managers should aspire to be. Best of all, this book spells out exactly how to develop those critical leadership skills, no matter where you are in your career. In my experience leading HR in several industries and companies, a resource like this is invaluable to leadership development."

Erin McSweeney

EVP, Chief Human Resources Officer, Optum

"Now more than ever, leaders must be agile - able to respond to ever changing market conditions and employee needs and expectations. The Rise of the Agile Leader is a practical handbook to help you improve your leadership skills and effectiveness. Our goal as leaders must be to drive employee engagement and alignment with the strategy, and Chuck Mollor gives us a roadmap to true talent optimization."

Kirk Arnold

Executive in Residence, General Catalyst. Senior Lecturer, MIT Sloan School of Management

"A phenomenal read, fueled by deep personal experiences as well as decades of observing and advising the C-suite. This book invites you to self-reflect and be honest with yourself and in return offers numerous practical and actionable frameworks for being an increasingly effective and agile leader."

Gérard van Spaendonck

Managing Director and Operating Partner, JLL Partners

"The Rise of the Agile Leader is the blueprint for leaders during this immense changing landscape for organizations and more importantly, leaders transforming their leadership abilities overnight. The book takes you through a personal assessment that clearly assists you in elevating your approach to your teams and the changes they are experiencing. A successful leader will find pearls of wisdom along with tactical methodologies to assess the changes we are experiencing globally with remote working, jeopardized personal safety, and organizational changes coming faster than we can manage. Leaders will not get enough of this self-reflective read."

Sandra Sims-Williams

SVP, Diversity & Inclusion, Nielson

"I'm a believer in empowering teams and creating an environment in which people can do their best work. While that's not always easy in a constantly changing world, Chuck's coaching method and Agile Leader model has drastically enhanced the way I approach leadership and understand myself. Seeing the positive impact of putting his advice and models into action opens a new level of personal and professional achievement."

Kevin Manzolini

Vice President & GM of Consumer Electronics, Bose Corporation

"Chuck Mollor is a first-class coach who offers his years of helpful advice in this easy-to-read text. Being an Agile Leader is a must for this era of great change we are in and the even greater change that lies ahead. Chuck offers invaluable insights and wisdom on how to make this transition."

Thomas H. Grape

Chairman and CEO, Benchmark Senior Living

"If you're wondering what the future of leadership is and when will it arrive, you missed it. As Chuck mentions up front, 'the future is here'. The paradigm has already shifted and the workplace is filled with people and teams with different expectations, lifestyles, values, and commitment levels. The Rise of the Agile Leader prepares you to lead with consciousness, vulnerability, and a deeper understanding of yourself and your teams. Chuck Mollor provides a succinct narrative and the practical models and systems that will start you on your transformation into your own version of an agile leader."

Matt Monkiewicz

President & CEO, Kayem Foods

"Agility has been proven to be one of the most essential skills a leader can have, especially in today's rapidly changing world. I've worked with hundreds of HR and business executives throughout my career, and one of the most elusive skills is how to develop effective leadership capabilities, particularly as people move into C-suite positions. The Rise of the Agile Leader distills this into an approachable and digestible format. I'd recommend this highly engaging book to anyone looking for a practical way to foster agility in themselves or their teams."

Tracy Burns
CEO Northeast Human Resource Association (NEHRA),
Co-Founder Hytched

"I wish I'd had this book when I started my career because of the sheer number of "aha" moments it provides. But as a CEO, I find it equally valuable in helping me navigate the ever-changing marketplace and thoroughly understanding my people's needs, as well as my own. Chuck's models, tools, and methodologies leave no stone unturned when it comes to how to build your own self-awareness and use it as your superpower to maximize your organization's potential. A great read for leaders of today and tomorrow."

Michael J. Reynolds
Chief Executive Officer, Farm Credit East

"We all face complex business challenges in our roles, but those who provide straightforward solutions are most successful. That's exactly what Chuck Mollor delivers in this book. I'm focused on talent and results – Chuck's model and tools equip current and aspiring leaders to maximize both. By bringing your whole self, being deeply emotionally intelligent, and checking your ego at the door, leadership success is within your reach!"

Sarah Goggin
Chief People Officer, Staples Stores

"The Rise of the Agile Leader is an engaging and candid narrative about Chuck's personal experiences and how they shaped him as a leader. The book invites you to take a critical look in the mirror to reflect on what you can be doing better as a leader and backs it up with pragmatic concepts and tools to move you and your organization forward. Having worked with Chuck and his team at MCG Partners, I know he is passionate about his work, the tools and techniques that he recommends to his clients, and building stronger leaders and high-performing teams. The Rise of the Agile Leader is a must-read for executives looking to grow."

Brad Wright

CEO, Cambridge Systematics

"The Rise of the Agile Leader is well-timed in today's ever-changing macro environment and is delivered with practicality and rare simplicity. Chuck Mollor breaks down the components of Agile Leadership into an identifiable set of behaviors, allowing readers to understand their own tendencies and how they're perceived by teams and organizations. Along the way, Chuck shares his own journey, experiences, and key "aha" moments that bring these lessons to life. Anyone in a position of leadership or aspiring to be can glean insights from this book to help become a better version of themselves in service to others."

Scott Daley

Vice President, Footwear, Reebok International,

an Adidas Company

"As an advocate for servant leadership, I've always believed that a leader's greatest asset is their people. This book clearly demonstrates how agile leaders empower their people to drive business success and do so authentically and sustainably. Insightful, articulate, and precise, The Rise of the Agile Leader is a must-read for leaders at every level."

Ed Manzi

Chairman and CEO, Fidelity Bank

"The Rise of the Agile Leader accelerated my development by opening my eyes to the impact of strategic leadership. Since incorporating purposeful awareness and development of myself and my teams, we're operating more strategically, able to pivot more quickly, and driving innovation more effectively. As someone who's benefitted immensely from the agile leadership framework, I recommend this book to anyone ready to unlock their potential impact."

Lei Zhang
Global Head of Software and Systems, Automotive,
Bose Corporation

"While there is no shortage of books on the topic of leadership, Chuck has managed to create a very unique and contemporary book. Chuck blends a deep 'empirical' body of research with his own rich personal and professional experiences to create compelling framework for self-exploration and leadership growth. I'm struck by the pragmatism of the work born from more than 30 years of having a 'birds eye view' on leaders and the impact they have, both positive and negative, on the organizations they lead. You will pick up more than a few gems here".

Marc B. Reuss
EVP & Chief Human Resources Officer, Excelitas Technologies

"If you are responsible for identifying, hiring, managing, or leading top talent, this book is for you. Chuck Mollor makes a strong case for why your people are an organization's most valuable resource and how to foster a culture that allows them to perform to their potential. As someone who has been focused on getting the right leaders into growing organizations for more than 20 years, I recommend this book and would advise any current or future leader to read it as well."

Alice Koehn Benson
CEO, Benson Executive Search

"It's during times of uncertainty that great leaders emerge. But how can leaders evolve and adapt to meet the demands of this new world of work? For leaders, these demands can be both overwhelming and daunting. The leadership strengths that have served us well in the past are unlikely to predict our success in the future. The pace of change and the expectation to build amazing teams and drive impactful business outcomes requires leaders to think differently and relentlessly adapt. The Rise of the Agile Leader gives leaders the toolkit they need to elevate their leadership capabilities, adapt their style and create amazing outcomes. Chuck Mollor shares his experiences as a management consultant, executive coach, entrepreneur, son, and father to personalize the journey of leadership. He gives real world examples, practical capability models, and actionable tips that will lead to better team engagement, a robust culture, and measurable leadership success. This book is a great how-to for anyone who aspires to be a great leader. There has never been a better time for a book like this. "

Jill Larsen

Chief People Officer, PTC

"As an HR, culture, and leadership development expert, I've found few resources as elaborate as The Rise of the Agile Leader that adequately express the impact of leadership adaptability and a culture-first mindset. Chuck's methodologies can be quickly adopted by leaders in every industry to see immediate positive change throughout their organizations, and to ensure they maintain a strong, healthy culture that motivates their people every day. I've had the pleasure of working with Chuck Mollor on several occasions, he is known for his ability to inspire others to rediscover their purpose and ignite goal-achieving action. He has a natural ability to connect with people and he is a consummate professional who knows how to accelerate positive change."

Marianne Scaffidi

Chief People and Culture Officer, BBX Sweet Holdings

"Perfect for these unpredictable times when agile leadership is essential, Chuck Mollor's book is a must read for everybody who has a leadership role or aspires to get one. Read this book to get access to the distilled experience of an outstanding executive coach who generously shares the recipe for the secret sauce of effective agile leadership."

Irina Anghel-Enescu

Managing Director & Board Member, South Eastern European Private Equity and VC Association (SEEPEA)

"The learning quest of leadership is a gift to anyone who has the interest, the persistence, the open-mindedness, and the ability to reinvent her or himself. Moreover, it is about the agility to continuously search for new ways of empowering your emotions and those you lead, grounded in your values. Chuck Mollor has played a critical part in my leadership journey, and this book is a wonderful, thoughtful, and very practical expression of his wisdom about leadership and his coaching. I am sure you will enjoy the read."

Remco J. Steenbergen

Chief Financial Officer, Barry Callebaut Group

"This is an engaging read that offers a rich mix of self-reflection and pragmatic counsel on the principles of leadership. While many aspects of leadership are classic and stand the test of time, today's dynamic business environment requires that leaders be sensitive to shifting demands and able to inspire others to be nimble and highly adaptive to change. The concepts that Chuck Mollor articulates are applicable at any stage of your career, from new manager to the C suite. I find it useful to select a concept that can raise my game as a leader and apply the insights from this book to practice and built that new skill. I highly recommend this book!"

Kate Holzhauser

Vice President, Environmental, Health, Safety and Security, Chevron Phillips Chemical

"Chuck Mollor is one of the top thinkers today on the topic of leadership! This book is a must-read for every leader at each stage of their career. Full of wisdom and practical advice."

Doug Fletcher

Founder, Fletcher & Company. Co-author, *How Clients Buy*

"Chuck's book is an exercise in introspection. It's a reminder to me of the importance of being self-aware as a leader while reinforcing the importance of being authentic and true to who you are while being situational in your leadership and communication style based on your audience. If there's anything you take away from this book, it is that being able to adapt to an agile leadership style is not a destination, it's a journey - especially in today's uncharted business environment."

Nikhil Hunshikatti

Vice President, Acquisitions, Consumer Marketing, Gannett

Preface

"When the human spirit is moved and united with purpose, anything is possible." – Chuck Mollor

I'm very proud and excited to share with you my passion, insights, and lessons learned from years of advising, coaching, and developing leaders and their businesses. I will be sharing with you some of my own personal experiences and my vision for the future of leadership. I was one of those executives that didn't understand leadership and wasn't effective as a leader, and this book will highlight what I did to overcome that.

I will be going over my methodologies and best practices in what it takes to be a successful leader in life, your community, and in organizations.

You might be considering management or are early in your career as a manager. Maybe you are in middle management trying to advance, or someone who is ready to become a C-level executive, or you're already a C-level executive who wants to get to the next level of effectiveness.

You may be a manager struggling to find your leadership voice and potential. You may be trying to become an active participant in your community, in your school, or in your family.

Find what's important to you. Don't be afraid to look deep inside; reflect and be honest with yourself on what you need to do, and the patterns of feedback you have received in your lifetime. Make the time for this. Change and improve your leadership capability and life.

It's my hope for you to become inspired and committed, as I have, to change the world, one leader at a time, one day at a time. I've been on a journey to become my best, which then became my journey for you to become your best.

Acknowledgment

I dedicate this book to all those on their journey of self-discovery, exploring what leadership means for you, for others, and for organizations.

A very grateful thank you to my collaborators in writing and publishing this book - my publisher, Suzanne Doyle-Ingram; my editor, Michelle Barry; my marketing consultant, Dorree Gurdak; and Adrienne Mollor.

A special thank you to so many for their input and contributions over the years, especially my colleague, Cheryl Jacobs. Cheryl has been an outstanding friend and colleague and has helped me build MCG Partners from its very early days. A special thank you to Heather Wood for her lead role in our research and development of the Agile Leader model. To Erinne Tripp for her passion as resident PI Guru; and to Stephanie Holmgren for her positivity and let's do it work ethic. Other colleagues I would like to thank are: Nancy Martini, Frank Dadah, Liz Eskenazi, Riley McDonough, Josh Perlman, Steve Stulck, Roxana Pupkin, Mary Putnam, Joel Stanley, Alida Zweidler-McKay, Ryen McGinn, John Griffith, and so many more.

A special thank you to my partners, friends, collaborators and thought leaders at The Predictive Index, especially Mike Zani, Daniel Muzquiz, Matt Poepsel, Drew Fortin, Maribel Olvera, Rabih Shanshiry, and Josh Combest.

I'm very fortunate to have many sources of inspiration. Frank and Sandy Labate, may they rest in peace, were my "second parents" while growing up. Their sons - my best friend and "brother," Frank Labate, Jr., and his brother, Chris Labate, were family to me in my youth, and their extended family always made me feel welcomed and accepted. Frank Labate, Jr. and I were the best of friends growing up. We went through a lot together and have great memories playing sports, counseling at summer camp, and having crazy fun. I want to recognize my Aunt Helen and my grandmother/Omi, Ingeborg Hesse, may they both rest in peace. Linda Kravitz has been a wonderful friend and grandmother. She has been a role model as a 9th-degree black belt teaching my children karate, as a business owner, and as a progressive scientific mind, having earned a degree in chemistry and physics in a time when many women didn't pursue the sciences. She has been a wonderful supporter to our family, and we are so very grateful. Stanley Kravitz has been a great friend and role model. He has demonstrated to all of us how to live one's life with passion, curiosity, hard work, humility, and generosity. He is a modern renaissance man, an armed forces veteran and purple heart recipient, upholstery craftsman, health inspector, town selectman, general contractor and builder, precious metals professional, and a farmer; from chickens to cranberries, and being part of the Ocean Spray Co- operative, his greatest passion.

There are many family members, friends, teachers, and colleagues. You are all in my heart and mind, and I am very thankful to you and your impact. Special acknowledgment to Msgr. James McDermott (may he rest in peace), Coach Don Larkin (may he rest in peace), Professor Marguerite Kane, John Harris, Linda Sawyer, Erik Liebegott, Rob Fandel, Jenn Ryalls, Cliff Farrah, Paul Winch, Lisa Winch, Mark O'Connell, Carl Shishmanian, Andrew Sexeny, Dave Ricci, Kirsten Zwicker Young, Gary Young, Derek Wolkowicz, Candace Wolkowicz, Rick Gatto, Kristen Veitch, Dana Savoie, Chris Sears, Joe Freiday, Tom Rooney, Craig Medeiros, Scott Turner, Ed Buiser, Brian Buckley, Scott Hayward, Kevin Costa, Moftah El-Ghadi, Bruce Delle Chiaie, Ken Gad, Mike Hugyo, Dave Askew, Tom Rogers, Dennis Lyons, Joe Gilbody, Jonathan White,

Chuong Pham, Mike Macedo, Dave Hobaica, John Connor, Jeff Fruzzetti, Andy Corbett, Joe Ranahan, Mike Renzi, Dan Traer, Jamie McKenna, Mark Vatkevich, Bob Mather, Chris Grant, Douglas Ng, Ray Joyce, Ted Fleming, Paul Perdigao, cousin David Hesse, Auntie Laurie Wessels, nephews Jeff, Sean and Brian Lowe, nieces Jessica and Michelle Trussell, and cousins Don Huizer, Kathy Forbes, and Linda Morgan. Much of my inspiration comes from my mother, Rosemarie Strauch. I am very thankful to her wonderful husband, Don Strauch, and my sisters, Mary Lowe and Eileen Trussell.

My children, Lindsey, Stephanie, Annika, and Spencer Mollor, have given me so much meaning in my life. They showed me what dedicating your life to others really meant. Watching them grow, develop, and flourish has been such a blessing and a gift. I'm so very proud of them, and the wonderful people they have become. They share integrity, honesty, passion for life and learning, and demonstrate respect and love to others. They want to make the world a better place.

Lastly, to my ex-wife, Adrienne Mollor. She supported me and our family over the years. She is an amazing mother and friend. I'm very fortunate to have been with her and I appreciate how she helped me become a better person and professional. Thank you for believing in me.

Chapter 1: The Future of Leadership Is Now

I've been fortunate to have coached and advised many leaders, executives, and executive teams over the years. I've worked with people with very different backgrounds, expertise, industries, personalities, and styles. In this book, I will be sharing in greater detail how to understand yourself and others better, and why it's so critical to your future success. We will go over the dimensions of effective leadership and developing yourself as a leader—increasing leadership knowledge, techniques, and skills, in addition to behavioral modification. We will discuss why it's so important to understand what behaviors and reactions tend to get you into trouble, how you can modify your style without compromising authenticity or transparency, and why it's so critical to learn how to shift as a person and leader throughout your life. I call it *Agile Leadership*.

What is the future of leadership? My company and team spent over a year researching this topic, interviewing executives around the world, and speaking with our clients and thought leaders.

We learned that the future is already here and that your organization's survival is based on a number of key factors—including your ability to be agile. Through our research and expertise, we created a profile of the successful leader of today and of the future; a new leadership model, assessment, and development programs to identify and develop leaders to become an *Agile Leader*™. The following is an overview of our Agile Leader profile, along with the attributes and characteristics of what encompasses an Agile Leader.

Many companies are attempting agile transformation, but without the shift in traditional leadership mindset, abilities, and development, they will be unsuccessful. It's like putting a square peg into a round hole. Leaders need to be agile to develop and drive agile teams, organizations, culture, and results.

Considering how quickly market and competitive landscapes are shifting, agile organizations have a distinct advantage over more traditional organizational structures. Hierarchical, command-and-control structures are being replaced by dynamically constructed and reconstructed networks of teams. Modern organizations operate less like an assembly plant and more like living organisms—shifting, adopting, adjusting, and evolving.

A critical success factor in any agile transformation is the collective mindset and behaviors of its leaders. A shift to agile leadership requires new ways of thinking, interacting, and organizing. Attitudes and values must shift towards agile aims of experimentation, innovation, creativity, and flexibility. This shift demands skillful communication, commitment, and collaboration by leaders at all levels.

5 Key Drivers of Agile Leadership

The Agile Leader has the ability and capacity to assess risk soundly, decide courageously, and act quickly to meet a rapidly changing environment while producing results, and develop others' capacity to do the same.

We have identified five key drivers of Agile Leadership and ten leadership competencies that can be leveraged to change how organizations work and get work done.

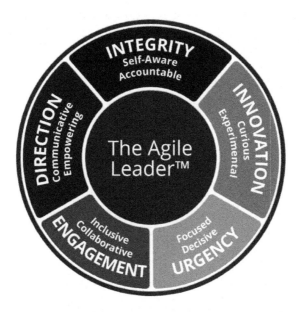

Source: MCG Partners

1. Integrity

Integrity is the foundation of agile leadership. Actions are driven by values and principles, which make leaders reliable and trustworthy. The Agile Leader has developed a depth of self-awareness, character, and purpose that naturally inspires those around them.

Integrity is the most important leadership attribute, but it's often overlooked or considered to be something that leaders simply have or don't have. But we believe that any leader can develop integrity. The combination of self-awareness and accountability accelerates the development of leaders, so their mindsets and behaviors are governed by principles of integrity.

2. Innovation

The Agile Leader must have an innovative approach. They exhibit a natural curiosity about their environments, introducing and encouraging new ideas and creating a learning culture.

The Agile Leader's role is less about commanding and controlling, and more about facilitating. Think of the Agile Leader as a curator or a gardener who invests in team growth. With an unrelenting commitment to serving customers, they are willing to challenge the status quo and drive change.

3. Urgency

The Agile Leader embodies a sense of urgency. They bring focus to the organization by establishing challenging goals and maintaining a steady cadence. They make decisions quickly with imperfect data to keep the organization moving forward.

Agile leaders decentralize decision-making by abandoning hierarchy in favor of self-organizing, cross-functional teams. Leaders who follow the discipline of talent optimization know that selecting an organizational structure that supports the business strategy—and then updating that structure as needed—is key to success.

4. Engagement

The Agile Leader creates engagement across the organization. They are inclusive across boundaries, generations, and geographies. They span up, out, across, and down complex networks of stakeholders to encourage cross-functional collaboration to generate optimal performance.

Another key to talent optimization is the idea of developing leaders at every level. Agile leaders pull multiple levers to build engagement in individual contributors, and they understand that engagement begets productivity.

5. Direction

The Agile Leader creates a direction for the organization and aligns people and resources to fulfill it. They focus on removing impediments and empowering teams to self-organize and take charge of their work. They are transparent in their communication and encourage a free flow of information to rapidly adapt to change.

10 Agile Leader Competencies

You may already possess some of the key attributes and characteristics of the Agile Leader. If not, you can work on developing them further. Here are the ten Agile Leader competencies:

1. Self-Awareness

Understands own strengths, styles, spirit and character, and reveals this to others. Has and conveys a sense of purpose.

2. Accountable

Committed to doing the right things for the right reasons. Exhibits consistency of values, principles, and actions.

3. Inclusive

Broadly includes others in achieving results and embraces diverse and unique perspectives across a variety of demographics and geographic locations.

4. Collaborative

Works broadly with others, understanding the complex, interrelated network of stakeholders that relate to the business and leads in a way that takes these diverse interests into account. Supports productive interactions in and across the team.

5. Communicative

Establishes shared meaning across individuals, teams, and stakeholders through clear and transparent two-way exchange of information. Links day-to-day efforts to larger organizational directions.

6. Empowering

Establishes an environment where employees can take charge of their work, self-organize, and adapt to changing demands.

7. Focused

Establishes and maintains a focus on achievement, demonstrating stamina and energy in pursuit of results, and encourages others to embrace shared goals.

8. Decisive

Integrates information from multiple sources to establish frameworks for decision-making and to make judgments quickly for continued progress.

9. Curious

Curious about customers, social trends, technology, and the market. Open to thinking differently and oriented to innovations that can improve client/customer experience or operations.

10. Experimental

Emphasizes growth through pushing limits, small experiments, and risk-taking to succeed in a volatile, uncertain, complicated, and unpredictable world.

The Agile Leader can tap into these competencies depending on the situation to create an agile culture based on shared organizational values that align your business and people strategies. Do you want a high-performing and engaged workforce? Do you want an organization that is aligned with your purpose, vision, and strategies?

If so, become an Agile Leader. This book will show you how.

Determine Your Agility

These five key drivers of agile leadership and the ten Agile Leader competencies are identifiable, observable, and measurable behaviors that are critical for a leader's success.

As you read through these, ask yourself these questions:

- Am I already an Agile Leader?
- Is my leadership team agile?
- What do I need to do to be more agile?
- How can I help my team become more agile?
- What does my organization need to do to be more agile?
- How do I create an agile culture?

I recommend you assess yourself by these four agile leadership attributes for yourself, your team(s), and your organization.

1. Self-Awareness

How aware are you of your natural leadership attributes and strengths? Organizations that practice talent optimization know that self-awareness helps leaders at all levels establish emotional intelligence. How do you perform under pressure and stress? How would you rate your ability to work effectively with a variety of different people and situations?

2. Accountability

Are you taking ownership of your responsibilities and results? Are all members of your team and organization holding themselves accountable?

3. Challenging the Status Quo

Are you having courageous dialogue, asking the tough and unpopular questions? Are you curious and comfortable in challenging the norms and killing the sacred cows?

4. Decisiveness

Are you able to make decisions, even if you don't have 100% of the data? Are you able to take risk and pivot in a new direction?

Being an Agile Leader managing agile teams in an agile organization can be overwhelming in a world of chaos, constant speed, and change.

How critical is it to be an Agile Leader? The world is changing. Leaders have to take quick, decisive action, pivot, and change. **An Agile Leader creates a safe and stable environment that allows experimentation, risk, and failure without repercussion.**

There are some people who are naturally more agile than others, but anyone can learn agile leadership. What will you do to become an Agile Leader? How will you create and develop Agile Leaders, teams, and organizations? The future is now.

Chapter 2: My Story

"No one can be authentic by trying to imitate someone else." – Bill George

Our leadership journey must include reflection upon how we each became who we are and how this is a foundational component to our path forward. Discovering your *authentic leadership* requires a commitment to developing yourself. You must devote yourself to a lifetime of realizing your potential. The journey to authentic leadership begins with understanding the story of your life. Your life story provides the context for your experiences, and through it you can find the inspiration to make an impact on the world. What have been the transformative experiences that gave meaning to your life? The following is a brief glimpse of several moments of my life story and how I rose above challenges and found my passion to lead and to develop leaders through coaching and advising executives.

Before Leadership

We all have a story of how we got to where we are in life today. It began when I was very young. My mother met my father in Switzerland. She was a nurse for a man who was from northern New Jersey and was living in Switzerland. She was caring for this man because he had polio. The man who would eventually become my father was friends with this man, and one day he came to visit him. That's when he met my mother.

My father courted my mother for two years, traveling back and forth from New Jersey to Switzerland, before asking her to marry him. They married in Switzerland and soon after, they moved to northern New Jersey, the place where my father had been living since he was a teenager. Originally born in Austria, my father Ernie came from a working-class, blue-collar family. My father was in the Navy and his older brother Joe was a Marine who fought in the Korean War. My mother, on the other hand, was from a family from the arts in Europe. Her father was Dr. Rudolf Hesse, an opera and theater director, and her brother Dr. Volker Hesse is an accomplished theater producer and director. My mother had a twin sister who became a nun, Schwester Antonia Hesse (may she rest in peace).

In a span of three-and-a-half years, my parents had three children. I was their first, then my two younger sisters came along. When I was two-and-a-half-years old, my father was tragically killed in a car accident. He was instantly killed by a drunk driver. My mother was then left to raise three very young children without money or a job, and she didn't speak English, so she had to take classes to learn English. She ended up working in retail for Macy's as she couldn't transfer her nursing credentials to the U.S., and she didn't have the money to get certified here. Eventually, she ended up working at a dental office for many years, and then went back to her roots when she "retired" to become a "hospice" companion and helper for those very ill or dying at their homes.

Raising three kids on her own is only one of the reasons why my mother is a pretty amazing person. If you met her, you would think she's had the most wonderful, charmed life. She is always full of life, energy, passion, and positivity. Yet, her life was far from that. She and her family lost everything during World War II and at one point were looking for food to eat on the streets, knocking door to door. She and her twin sister lived in an orphanage for several years in Europe before their mother was able to get them back.

A year after losing her husband (my father) in the car accident, she lost her stepfather, with whom she was very close, to a heart attack. Another year-and-a-half later, as my mother was hanging laundry on the small balcony on the second floor of a two-family home she rented, the railing snapped, and she fell onto the paved driveway below. At the time, I was five and my sisters were four and three. I remember walking to the edge of the balcony and seeing my mother below. Though she was injured, all my mother cared about was making sure I wouldn't fall too. I remember her yelling, "Someone get my son, so he doesn't fall!"

She spent the next several months in the hospital, and the doctors weren't sure if she would ever walk again. They performed radical surgery for that era, implanting a bone into her back, and she was on crutches for a year.

My mother is an incredible person who has overcome so many obstacles. Yes, she's had rough days, but she always kept her focus on her children, her family, her faith, and her closest friends. She stood by my side during a very shaky, and at times challenging, childhood. I had many ups and downs, but she was always there for me.

My mother has been a tremendous source of inspiration. Her unbelievable fight and resilience, her ability to not allow herself to be a victim of her life's circumstances while being so positive and enjoying the life she has is the example I aspire to every day. I'm so grateful to her, and I thank her for doing everything she could to give us a fighting chance.

I wasn't given a choice to where I went to high school. At home, I was a handful and needed more structure and discipline. I struggled for the first two years. I was frustrated and felt sorry for myself and the life I was handed. At my high school, if you failed a course, you were done. I failed a course as a sophomore and at the end of the school year, I was called into the principal's office expecting the obvious. But then a remarkable thing happened. The principal and dean of the school looked at me and told me they believed in me; that they were going to give me a second chance, assuming I went to summer school and passed the course I had failed. I left that meeting stunned.

All summer, I contemplated the impact of that conversation and decision by these two adults to bend the rules and give me an opportunity to prove myself. I became angry at myself. I realized that I had been blaming everyone around me for my problems instead of taking ownership for my part in them. It was one of several pivotal moments in my life, and it helped me get onto a better path in life, but my self-created challenges were far from behind me.

I finished high school on a better note, and I had a good college experience. Going into college I thought I wanted to become a lawyer, but my political science courses just weren't connecting with me and when I began speaking to professionals that were attorneys, I realized it wasn't for me. There were too many restrictions, rules, and protocols. It just was too limiting for me.

I then took a business policy course and the light bulb went off. I was intrigued by the different dynamics of how a business is run and wanted to learn more about solving business problems and how to build a successful business. I loved it and pursued management consulting right out of school due to the ability to work with many industries and address a variety of organizational and business challenges. But I was far from being a mature and responsible person. I went on to struggle with relationships, trying to find out who I was, and my purpose in life.

My Leadership Story

I was always curious. I liked to solve problems, fix things, and help others. How could I make this into a career? I wasn't sure. I was still trying to find my purpose.

I began my career experimenting with different types of jobs, such as process re-engineering consulting, human resource consulting, mergers and acquisitions, and change management. I was fortunate to travel around the world in these experiences, gaining exposure to many different cultures, industries, companies, and businesses. Along the way, I witnessed many organizational challenges. I worked for well-established, very large organizations as well as startups, and was involved in several restructures, mergers, and acquisitions.

As I approached my early thirties, I decided to join a very small talent management consulting firm. I was attracted to the job and company because I had the opportunity to build my own practice within the firm. I remember this time vividly. I had taken a 70% pay cut, moving from a large firm to take on this opportunity, but I had the ability to make a percentage of the business I brought in and delivered on. I was given a desk and a phone (this is 1995, before cell phones and the internet) and was told, "Good luck."

Despite my excitement and eagerness, I had very little success in my first year. It wasn't long before I started to have some doubts about whether this had been the right move. The owner of the firm must have sensed this because he sat me down to discuss how things were going. I told him that I wasn't sure if we should continue. He decided to give me more time, and he wanted to see the outcome from my first year. Timing is everything, and at the end of that year, the economy was heating up and my hard work began to pay off.

That chance my boss gave me reaped huge rewards for him, the firm, and me. By my fifth year, I had built an $8 million consulting practice. But in the wake of that success, a funny thing happened to me. I was making a lot of money, more than I expected I would make, but I wasn't happy.

I sat down with the owner over dinner one night and asked if he would be interested in possibly selling the firm to me someday, or in bringing me on as an equity partner. He very respectfully said, no, he was going to keep the firm. He wanted it to remain family owned and I understood his decision. But to his great surprise and shock, I then told him that I probably wouldn't be with the firm in a year. I was trying to be honest with him, as he'd been with me, but I knew my unhappiness was a sign that I needed to take on new responsibilities and challenges. I was too restless and unfulfilled in my role.

Through this experience, I learned something new about myself: the opportunity to take on new challenges and to develop new skills were more important to me than the money. So, it was no surprise when, almost a year after that fateful dinner, I joined a firm that had offered me an exciting new venture. I walked away from the significant financial windfall at the consulting firm to take on another startup opportunity. I started at a fraction of the salary I had been making, but at a global talent management firm and with the opportunity to learn and grow.

After a year of building up the business from the ground floor, the firm decided to merge with a sister company, which meant I was suddenly without a job. It was a surprising and humbling experience. But regardless of how it ended, I did have the good fortune to work with many talented people and learned a great deal about running and building a national and global consulting business.

At times I look back and chuckle. I spent my twenties and thirties trying to prove to the world how smart and hard-working I was, and how much potential I had. Then, I spent my forties trying to demonstrate my developed expertise and capabilities. By the time I reached my fifties, I realized how little I really knew and how much I still needed to learn.

At this point, I was running a large global practice that was very successful. I was a successor to the CEO. Everything seemed to be going my way. But one day, the CEO asked me if I'd ever had a 360° assessment. I said no and asked him why.

He smiled and said, "Let's see what the results will be."

The feedback from my key stakeholders (boss, peers, subordinates, and others) through the 360-degree assessment was painful. It was similar to experiencing the stages of grief: shock, denial, anger, bargaining, depression, and acceptance. The CEO gave me some difficult critiques as well, but I needed to hear it. I eventually realized that my lack of self-awareness of how I saw myself versus how others experienced me was the size of the Grand Canyon.

At that time, my maturity level meant that my initial reaction was, "Screw them! Look how hardworking and successful I am."

My CEO and boss smiled, knowing I would react this way.

All he said was, "Chuck, you will always be successful in life. You work hard, you overcome obstacles, you surround yourself with talented people, and you get results. You care about people and you are likable. However, if you want to be in my seat one day, you need to learn leadership. You are a good manager, but you don't yet get leadership."

It was a surprise to hear this. At first, I wasn't sure what he meant about not getting leadership, but I began to walk down a path to understand what that meant for me. He sent me on my way, with the assignment to, "Go think about it for a few days," and then we would talk again.

So, I went away, got over myself, and then returned to let him know he was right. Once I got over the shock of the negative feedback, I realized that I needed to learn and understand what leadership was, and what it was for me. Most of all, I was ready to learn what it would take for me to become a successful leader. That became another significant transformational moment in my life, just like the principal who'd decided to give me a chance all those years ago.

Another important experience happened about a year later. I hired a friend/colleague to help me evaluate and assess our global salesforce. I was looking to shift our capability from a purely rela-tionship-focused approach to be more of a consultative approach and skill set. This required us to evaluate our current salesforce and get a better understanding of their overall sales skills and behav-ioral profiles. We wanted to assess whether our sales team had the ability to grow and develop into more consultative sales profes-sionals.

As my friend and consultant that I'd hired began to assess, de-velop, and train the sales team, I mentioned my leadership team had some challenges. We were not aligned and had conflicts. As a result, the team had difficulties with making decisions, hearing everyone out, and dealing with the "elephant in the room." She suggested that we take an assessment she used called The Predictive Index Behavioral Assessment™ (PI).

At the time, I was not a big fan of behavioral assessments; I had been skeptical in the past of them and their results. I'm not sure if you've ever had this experience but I would read a question in the assessment/survey and had to choose an answer, usually between A and E. Often, I would agree with 80% of one answer and 20% of another, and would walk away saying, "how accurate can this be if I don't agree with all of my answers?" I was never shown a good reason for how assessments would be helpful to me, my team, or my organization and hadn't experienced positive results from other assessments.

An organization can use PI throughout the "talent management life cycle." Managers can implement PI to hire, onboard, manage, build and align teams, develop leaders and successors, engage em-ployees, and manage change, integrations, restructures, and mer-gers and acquisitions. It can also help employees understand what's the right role, culture, and career path for them, and how to work more effectively in teams.

Source: Chuck Mollor

With the PI behavioral assessment, I had a very different experience from assessments I'd taken in the past. It's a free-choice survey, meaning I could choose any answers I wanted, instead of a forced-choice survey. However, when I first received my PI behavioral profile report, my first reaction was, "This isn't me."

My consultant and friend looked at me and said, "Chuck, how many years have I known you? This is you." We shared a laugh.

Looking back, I did need to be hit between the eyes to jolt me a bit, so I revisited the report and overcame my inability to see myself very accurately and my initial skepticism (level of skepticism— something PI provides insight to as well). When I looked at my PI behavioral profile the next day, I began to internalize what I was reading. I then reflected on the 360° assessment feedback I had received a year earlier, and it clicked. I could see the correlation between how people experienced me (my 360) and who I was (PI). As my friend and consultant walked me through my PI behavioral profile, I began to understand what happens to me under pressure and stress; how I overuse my strengths, which derails my ability to be effective. After these experiences, I went from the big skeptic of behavioral assessments to drinking the Kool-Aid. It opened my eyes not just to myself, but to understanding the behavioral characteristics and traits of my team members, and why at times we were not aligned and struggling.

PI helped me understand and *accept* the people around me. Here is a story to illustrate this: When I was running that big practice in my late thirties, my core team and I were meeting in a conference room and I was passionately articulating our vision and strategy, and how we were going to overcome mountains and take that hill. I even pounded my fist onto the table. I remember there were a few people at the firm who were wired like me; they were just as excited and passionate as I was. But there were also a few people who had that "deer in the headlights" look; they were looking at me as if I were a freight train rumbling at them at 250 miles an hour, the ground shaking, the horn blaring, and the light shining in their eyes.

I recall becoming frustrated and saying to myself, "Why are they being like that?" It didn't dawn on me until I took the PI behavioral assessment that I realized they weren't trying to shut down when I was behaving like that. They were being their true selves. My issue was that I was not adjusting my style to my audience! Those that were shutting down with the "glazed donut" eyes were overwhelmed by my intensity, assertiveness, and tone. What I needed to do, and have learned to do since, is slow down; speak at a more measured pace and tone. Yes, I can be passionate, but in a more measured way. Instead of yelling and pounding on the table, connect with each person in the room, smile, and most importantly, ask questions; facilitate dialogue. Most likely, the team members in that meeting had many of the opposite traits, behaviors, and characteristics that I naturally have. They are more accommodating than assertive; they are calmer and more deliberate than intense and driving. *I needed to speak their language instead of forcing them to speak mine.*

You might be saying to yourself, well, the example above isn't me or I can't relate to some or all of that. For some of us that will be true, but the question is, what behaviors do you need to modify depending on your audience to be more effective?

Since discovering the benefits of PI, I have completely pivoted my way of thinking and dedicated myself to improving self-awareness and self-acceptance. We will discuss this *two-sided coin* later on in the book. Ever since that day, I've been on a mission to learn the difference between leadership and management and discover what's needed to become a more effective leader in a whole new world of work. Eventually, I did sit in the CEO seat, when I ran and grew a successful global business.

But in 2007, I reached another important moment. I wasn't happy, I was traveling too much, and I was burnt out. I wasn't having fun anymore and knew I needed to make another significant change and shift. So right as the economy was about to collapse, I started my own firm, a leadership and talent optimization firm called MCG Partners.

After going through my own trials and tribulations as a leader and wanting to share my practical experiences in business, operations, sales, and management, becoming an executive coach made sense as my next step. So, that's what I did. I dove into the methodologies, skills, credentials, and certifications of becoming an executive coach and have been on that journey ever since.

In thinking about my goals with this firm, I wanted the best of both worlds. I knew I wanted to have more control over my schedule and my life so I could be around to raise my children and be an available and active husband, family member, and friend. I also wanted to get back to my roots in consulting and advising and to build a team of like-minded people.

If my colleagues who worked with me before I discovered PI knew that I would go on to become a successful executive coach, they would probably fall out of their chairs! I've come a long way as a person, as a leader, and as a coach. Now, I would like to share what I've learned with you.

If I can do it, so can you! In this book, I will show you how.

The journey and the quest continue—to make a difference in the world, to learn what leadership is for others and for me, and to become a more whole person. I am convinced that is my purpose, and importantly, it is my passion—to help leaders, teams, organizations, and businesses be successful.

It is my sincere hope that you are helped by this book. The information and strategies are applicable to anyone, whether you are a seasoned CEO, considering managing for the first time, somewhere in between, or if you're leading an organization and are trying to figure out how to create and sustain a leadership culture to develop a highly engaged and performing workforce.

Chapter 3: Can Anyone Be an Agile Leader?

"A good leader inspires people to have confidence in the leader; a great leader inspires people to have confidence in themselves." – Eleanor Roosevelt

Can You Be an Agile Leader?

Maybe you're already in management, or maybe you're considering a management role in the near future. You might be struggling to be successful as a manager or to advance your career in management. You may be asking yourself: *Can I be a leader?* Do I have the right knowledge, skills, or mindset for leadership? Do I have what it takes? Do I want to lead? Whether you're comfortable in your position or hoping for a promotion, it's likely that at some point these questions have crossed your mind.

You may be a top producer or expert in your profession, but that doesn't always translate to being a good leader. It takes much more than just a great track record and knowledge.

What does it take to be an effective leader in today's corporate world? Do you have to be authoritative, extraverted, or a risk-taker? Or, can you lead effectively if you're reserved, analytical, and risk-averse? What will change if you become a leader?

Years of research have shown that there is no single profile for leaders. Just like there are all kinds of public speakers, there are all kinds of leaders. Some are quiet, reserved, and analytical. Some are gregarious, assertive, and passionate. An authoritative person may be an excellent leader. A less assertive, more encouraging person can also be a very different kind of effective leader.

If you look at people who are considered the best leaders in the world, they are all very different, but they're very successful. Why?

It takes certain leadership qualities to be successful within certain organizational cultures. It also depends on what business cycle your organization is going through. Is your business experiencing significant growth, expansion, contraction, recession, or going through a shift? Is there a plan for restructuring, or maybe a merger or acquisition?

By using the right tools and framework and understanding how to be effective in a variety of situations, you can be a great leader, no matter what your approach, philosophy, or style may be.

What makes leaders successful despite their behavioral differences comes down to a few key things. The following are critical characteristics:

They have a great capacity for self-awareness. Great leaders know their strengths and weaknesses, and what gets them into trouble. They understand what happens to themselves under pressure and stress, and they realize the impact they have on others.

They have a clear purpose. Visionary leaders know what their purpose is and how to convey it. They are skilled at communicating the "why." They can explain the purpose, vision, mission, and strategy of what the team is working toward so everyone understands it and can identify with it.

They welcome and accept diversity in all its forms. Strong leaders understand the differences of others, and what motivates and drives people.

They have strong team-building skills. Successful leaders surround themselves with people who have strengths that complement theirs, leveraging capabilities they don't have themselves.

They are authentic. Inspiring leaders are consistent and true to who they are and what they believe, but they can also adjust their approach based on new data, and depending on who their audience is; they can modify their approach without feeling they have to modify who they are.

They have mentors and advisors. The best leaders don't go it alone. Even with their successes and accomplishments, they are always listening, learning, seeking input and counsel, and exploring options. They are externally focused and thinking about the future, constantly looking at best practices and trends. They know they don't know it all.

Management and Leadership - What's the Difference?

Most people use both terms interchangeably, but they are not the same. It's important to understand the distinctions between management and leadership, and to understand why *both* are more critical than ever. So, what's the difference?

You *manage* things, processes, and systems. You *lead* people.

Being a great leader has been a focus of mine for a number of years, including helping my clients shift from an authoritative-based management style (command and control) to engaging and empowering employees. "Management" took a back seat. Both managing and leading are critically important, but it's rare to be good at both. Some managers are naturally suited to be better managers than leaders, and some managers are more adept at leading than managing. We need to learn which we are more naturally effective in—managing or leading.

As previously mentioned, this can be done by using PI. Through assessment, improved self-awareness and development, you can determine whether you're naturally stronger in leading or managing, and what you need to do to be effective in both. You are then able to chart your course on how to develop yourself to be more effective. The following chart illustrates the differences:

Management	Leadership
Control	Trust/empowerment
Authority/hierarchy	Alignment and expertise
Discrete tasks	Focus on vision
One-way communication	Circular communication
Fear of risk	Experimentation
Dominating perspective	Inviting multiple perspectives
One decision maker	Team decisions
Measurement	Personal accountability
Quick decision making	Ensuring wise decisions
Tried and true	Innovation
Director	Coach and counselor

Looking at it another way...

Managers take care of where you are	Leaders take you to a new place
Managers deal with complexity	Leaders deal with uncertainty
Managers are efficient	Leaders are effective
Managers create policies	Leaders establish principles
Managers measure value	Leaders create value
Managers have subordinates	Leaders have followers
Managers create circles of control	Leaders create circles of influence

Without good managers, employees are less likely to be effectively trained, get their work done, and execute their plan of action. Without good leaders, employees will lose sight of why their work is important in the first place.

Leaders take a strategic, long-range view and keep employees aligned with the vision, mission, values, strategic goals, and leadership development of the organization. They handle questions like the following:

Vision. What is our vision of the future?
Mission. What is our business purpose?
Values. What values do we want to demonstrate?
Strategic Goals. What will take us into the future we envision?
Leadership. What are we doing to develop our future leaders?

Managers have to be tactical, taking a short-range view and focusing on processes, functions, and jobs. Their domain is questions like these:

Processes

- What must get done?
- With what measurable results?
- What are our key work processes?
- What are our customer and supplier requirements?

Functions

- Do our functions support our processes, organizational vision, and strategy?

Jobs

- Key Results
  - ☐ Do we know the demands of each job?
  - ☐ Do we have the right people in the right jobs?
  - ☐ What are the behavioral requirements of each job?
  - ☐ Are the jobs aligned with our vision, strategy, functional, and process goals?

Depending on where you are in your managerial career, being an effective manager or leader is not weighted equally. Early in your managerial career, most of your responsibilities will have a greater focus on being an effective manager. As you progress higher up the ladder, that will begin to shift. When you become a senior executive, most of your responsibilities will be about being an effective leader. This will require a sea of change in how you approach your role, and what your priorities will be.

Know Your Leadership Style

While there is no one style or profile for successful leaders, it is important to know yourself well enough to realize what your style is and how you can best work within that style.

Everyone has a dominant leadership style, a way that they tend to lead people. This can change in certain situations, particularly when under pressure or stress. Occasionally, a situation may arise where you will have to tap into a leadership style other than what is most comfortable for you. Perhaps you are a quiet, reserved leader but you are called on to give a motivational presentation that requires a bit more charisma and connection with your audience. Or, you may be an assertive, intense, and independent leader, but you need to adopt a calmer, more collaborative presence in order to deal with or interact with a particular member of your team.

Whatever your style or the occasion, there is no "best" leadership style. Instead, good leaders have a strong sense of self-awareness and the ability to assess the situation so they can respond with the right approach.

If you're not sure what your style is or how your personality translates into leadership, or that of your leadership team(s), there are many tools that can help you. In my executive coaching experience, I have had outstanding results working with leaders and leadership teams in their development, alignment, and success. One of the key platforms we use in our practice to increase self-awareness and the awareness of the styles of those we work with is PI.

The PI Behavioral Assessment™ is one of the more established and accurate behavioral assessments. Created in 1955 by Arnold Daniels, PI has some very distinct advantages and value propositions, which is why we use it with clients in our firm and emphasize it in this book. It is a powerful platform, not only for self-awareness but also for understanding how to be effective as a manager and leader, what your natural style is, and how you deal with different types of personalities. It's a foundational tool when it comes to understanding how to be a successful manager or management team, and how to be agile.

The PI Behavioral Assessment is a unique management tool that measures an individual's strengths, motivations, and behaviors. Why is this important? Exceptional performance is driven by the knowledge, experience, and skills an employee brings to the organization, but also by their behavioral style. The quality of how an employee performs in the job is also driven by leveraging their natural strengths and motivations, and how they interact with others and work within the culture of an organization. Utilizing the PI Behavioral Assessment to enhance a leader's self-awareness and understand how they leverage their management and leadership style, especially under stress and pressure, allows a leader a deeper understanding and awareness of how each leader:

- manages versus leads
- communicates
- builds relationships
- persuades and influences
- makes decisions
- delegates
- manages conflict
- deals with and manages change
- addresses risk and innovation
- acts as part of a team

The PI Behavioral Assessment is:

- Fast (7-minute assessment), simple (2.5-page report), and accurate
- Scientifically valid and reliable
- Agnostic to the user's age, gender, or race (Based on over 500 validity studies)
- Used by more than 10,000 large and small businesses in 150 countries and in more than 60 languages

No matter how you lead, lead well. Be aware that your style will help shape your team and the organization's culture.

Improving your self-awareness can have dramatic results. In a study of 486 publicly traded companies' stock performance, Korn/ Ferry International found that **companies with strong financial performance tend to have employees with higher levels of self-awareness than poorly performing companies.**[1]

---

[1] Korn Ferry Institute, June 2015

Leadership Framework

Once you've identified your leadership style, you need a framework by which to apply your style to the people in your organization. Some companies will provide a framework (I provided one earlier with *The Agile Leader*), but if you want to take responsibility for your own leadership development and success, you will need to adopt a model for yourself.

Effective leaders need a strong vision and an impactful strategy. They are expected to get things done. Leadership evaluations and studies often find that to be effective as a leader, and to have people engage with you as a leader, you need to be able to demonstrate the following seven qualities:

Care. *Put your people first.* Putting customers first is a popular slogan, but we can learn from winning CEOs like Virgin Group's Richard Branson and Zappos' Tony Hsieh, who have proven that putting the team first is what makes customers happy. It's common sense, isn't it? Fight for your people. Defend them. Protect them and take good care of them.

Care about who your people are, where they've come from, and what their ambitions and fears are. Take the time to understand your people—what keeps them awake at night, what gets them excited to start each day, and what motivates and drives them. Do you know what their passions and interests are? Do they feel comfortable sharing with you their ambitions and dreams? This takes more than a one-time conversation. Address what people need, which is not always what they want. Be sincere and direct, but also be sensitive and aware of how you provide feedback and input. Always ask the question, "How will my audience receive what I'm about to communicate?"

Demonstrate Empathy. Practice empathy. It helps us see a situation, a solution, or an idea from someone else's perspective. Imagine where others are coming from, what challenges and opportunities shape their thoughts. How do these perspectives shape bigger ideas? Pay attention to when they are struggling or going through a tough time. Show that you care.

Be Approachable. Being approachable is more than just having an open door. It's about *being present*—focus on who you are interacting with and not thinking about your next meeting, the problem you are trying to solve, or what is on your smartphone or laptop. *Listen*—ask probing questions so you clearly understand what you are hearing and can push a person's thinking; demonstrate *active listening* by stating back what you believe you heard. It's also about *being humble*—admitting what you don't know, when you are wrong, and the weaknesses you have. *Being open, receptive* about who you are, the experiences that have shaped who you are, and what is important to you, help build an environment of trust and openness.

> *"When you talk, you are only repeating what you already know. But if you listen, you may learn something new."* –Dalai Lama

Create a Safe Work Environment. Google completed a massive two-year study on team performance that revealed the one thing that the highest-performing teams have in common: *a safe work environment.* This is the belief that you won't be punished when you make a mistake or challenge decisions. Studies show that a safe work environment (*psychological safety*) allows for moderate risk-taking, speaking your mind, higher creativity, and sticking your neck out without fear of having it cut off—just the types of behavior that lead to market breakthroughs and internal and external innovation.

A safe work environment encourages people to ask questions, raise concerns, and challenge the status quo. As a result, employees are more open-minded, resilient, motivated, engaged, and persistent. A safe work environment increases humor, solution-finding, and divergent thinking. It helps create a place where there are no limits to what employees can bring to the table. In Google's fast-paced, highly demanding environment, creating and sustaining a safe environment has been the foundation of the company's success.

Develop Others. What are you doing to develop the next generation of leaders? How have you identified your top talent, and what is your plan on how to develop them? What is your succession methodology and plan? You know you have become a great leader when there are people who work for you who are better for your position than you are. You have helped them improve their skills, experiences, abilities, accomplishments, and careers. Most importantly, they now carry the torch you passed on to them by developing the next generation of leaders.

Walk the Talk. If you hold your people to a high standard of values, behaviors, and performance, and you do not demonstrate the same, you're being hypocritical. Do you want to create a high performing culture and have your people be engaged, committed, and focused? Be genuine, *walk the talk—demonstrate* the values, behaviors, and performance you expect of others.

Learn and Adapt. Be true to yourself and be your authentic self. At the same time, be open to self-improvement as a leader. *Be open to and ask for feedback and input.* Take the time each week for self-reflection and development. Ask yourself some of these questions: What have I learned about myself and others? How would I handle that situation differently next time? How can I effectively prepare for an upcoming meeting or decision?

What are you doing to ask others for input and feedback? Do you know your natural style and strengths, and those of the team you work with? How are you adjusting your approach to be more effective in working with others, in how you build relationships, influence and persuade, make decisions, and deal with conflict, risk, and change? **One of the greatest challenges of smart and successful people is to ask for feedback and adjust their formula for success.** Remember my story of the feedback from my CEO and my key stakeholders? You may think that you have followed a fail-proof method for success, but it's possible that your method could use improvement as the world around you is changing. Be willing to adapt as necessary.

Begin to find ways to practice what you've already learned. Keep learning, adapting, and changing. Knowing how and when to shift is an essential component of agile leadership.

Chapter 4: The Business Case for Leadership

What Does the Future Look Like for Leadership?

Leadership has never been more difficult. The world is evolving quickly, and many of us have a hard time keeping up with it. We are so connected that sometimes we feel like the world is in our backyard. All of its challenges, problems, and catastrophes feel unbelievably close.

We live in a fast-paced, ever-changing, disruptive time and it's not slowing down.

There are some startling examples and numbers. Compared to 18 years ago, 52% of Fortune 500 companies no longer exist, and it's anticipated that half of the current Fortune 500 won't be here in 10 years.[2]

About 75% of all venture capital-funded startups don't survive,[3] 33% of small businesses fail in their first year,[4] and only about 30% of family-owned businesses make it into the second generation.[5]

If that isn't concerning enough, CEO turnover rates reached a record high in recent years.

Not convinced that times have changed? Check this out:

- 21% of millennial workers say they've changed jobs within the past year[6]

---

[2] Harvard Business Review, "Digital Transformation Is Racing Ahead and No Industry Is Immune," July 2017
[3] Scale Finance, "The Venture Capital Secret - 75% of Startups Fail"
[4] Fortunly, "What Percentage of Small Businesses Fail," July 2019
[5] The Boston Globe, "More than 8 Out of 10 Family Businesses Have No Succession Plans," February 2018
[6] Gallup, "Millennials: The Job-Hopping Generation"

- Only half of millennials anticipate they'll still work at their company one year from now[7]
- As of 2020, millennials form 50% of the global workforce[8]
- Two out of three U.S. workers experience professional burnout[9]
- 85% of employees worldwide show some level of disengagement[10]

We are experiencing a time of rapid innovation and advances in technology, automation, and digitization.

Change management is no longer an initiative. It is a daily part of business and life. How can you keep up with all the changes in your role, with your people and your organization, your business, your competition, your customers, and with trends?

Mergers, acquisitions, restructures, transformations, reorganizations, integrations, decentralizations, and centralizations—they are happening more often than ever.

Consumers are constantly changing what they want and need, and their expectations have never been higher. No longer content with communicating during "business hours," they now demand 24/7 personalized service. Organizations are expected to know what their customers want and deliver it as quickly as possible. The so-called *Amazon Effect* means that consumers' expectations are higher than ever; they want it cheaper and they want it instantly.

We are living in a culture of now, where it's all about immediate satisfaction and gratification, and where trends and interests change in a nano-second.

---

[7] Gallup, "Millennials: The Job-Hopping Generation"
8 PWC, "Millennials at Work: Reshaping the Workplace"
9 Forbes, "Two-Thirds Of Workers Experienced Burnout This Year: How To Reverse The Trend In 2020," December 2019
10 Gallup, "Dismal Employee Engagement Is a Sign of Mismanagement"

There are more generations in the workforce than ever before. Much of this is due to how quickly generations are now developing. It used to be at least a decade before we saw a new generation; now, it's a few years. These generations have different views, expectations, and standards of what success looks like. They see their careers and lifestyles very differently from previous generations.

We work in a global environment where managers today are managing employees across geographies, time zones, countries, languages, and cultures. They are managing a *virtual workforce,* which requires a very different approach to connection, developing, guiding, and engaging.

The future of work is here. We're witnessing a massive shift from traditional work and full-time employment to freelancing, working part-time, and independent contracting. This is the *gig economy.* About 36% of U.S. workers are now involved in the gig economy and it's anticipated to grow to 50% in the next 7 years. The gig economy is expanding three times faster than the U.S. workforce as a whole.[11]

Social media and access to information have changed the world we live in. Opinions and views, uncensored, are right at our fingertips and influence how people think and view you, your organization, and your products and services.

Organizations and their leaders are more visible and public than ever. Tools like Glassdoor allow anyone to publicly evaluate a company and its leadership.

What are the implications? Organizations, teams, and employees need to be nimbler than ever, which means *leaders need to be agile to create agile teams and organizations.*

---

[11] SmallBiz Genius, "The Future of Employment – 30 Telling Gig Economy Statistics," August 2019

The markets of today and tomorrow reward organizations that have the capacity and willingness to adapt. Market leaders have established cultures and management approaches that encourage creativity and rapid innovation. These approaches, commonly referred to as agile, encourage leaders to pivot faster in response to our volatile, uncertain, complex, and ambiguous world.

Employee Engagement

Engagement is an individual's emotional commitment to his or her organization and its goals. Engagement is fueled by fit and satisfaction with one's job, manager, organization, and coworkers, and it manifests as discretionary effort at work. Discretionary effort is going above and beyond *minimum* job requirements. If employees put in "real" passion and extra hours into their work to make it something they're proud of, it results in increased productivity. It also means increased ownership and better results.

Engagement is linked to all sorts of positive impacts on employees and companies alike. For example, take a look at a recent Gallup report on employee engagement. **Companies with highly engaged workforces outperform their peers by 147% in earnings per share. They also see 20% higher productivity and 21% higher profitability.**[12]

The bottom line is: engagement matters.

So how is it that according to a recent Gallup's U.S. employee engagement survey, only about a third of American workers are engaged? What about that other two-thirds? Fifty-one percent are not engaged and 16% are actively disengaged.

---

[12] Gallup, "How Employee Engagement Drives Growth"

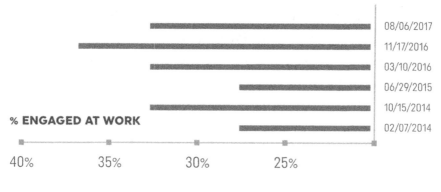

% ENGAGED AT WORK

	08/06/2017
	11/17/2016
	03/10/2016
	06/29/2015
	10/15/2014
	02/07/2014

40%   35%   30%   25%

Source: Gallup

Disengaged employees bring decreased productivity and decreased results. These employees are keeping you from achieving high performance and profitability. This is true whether they're trudging along or actively trying to leave.

As a leader, you can't ignore employee engagement, especially since engagement levels are tied to business revenue. Actively disengaged employees in the U.S. cost businesses $483 billion to $605 billion each year in lost productivity.[13] But productivity isn't the only disengagement "tax" on companies.

The effects of disengagement can be felt in:

- The ability to attract and hire great employees (disengaged employees may badmouth your company on sites like Glassdoor)
- Voluntary and involuntary turnover
- Stress and anxiety inflicted on peers and managers
- Your brand's reputation
- Customer satisfaction

---

[13] Newsday, "Small Business: Easy ways to measure employee engagement," October 2019

According to Harvard Business Review (HBR), studies have shown that disengaged workers have "37% higher absenteeism, 49% more accidents, and 60% more errors and defects." Actively disengaged employees also report more health problems. This includes high blood pressure, depression, and pain.

Disengaged workers exhibit a toxic ripple effect on their peers and teams. Another HBR study showed 78% of employees said their commitment to the organization declined in the face of toxic behavior. Sixty-six percent said their own performance declined.[14]

According to an Axial study, companies with high disengagement were 40 times less likely to identify their culture as a great place to work, compared to fully engaged employees. Disengagement is associated with lack of trust, increased bullying, lack of creativity, poor interpersonal relations, conflict, and loss of cultural values among many other negative effects.

Organizations with low employee engagement scores experienced 18% lower productivity and 16% lower profitability. They also saw 37% lower job growth and 65% lower share price over time.

Gallup found that 70% of the variance in team engagement is determined solely by the manager. Essentially, how effective the manager is.

Accelerate Employee Engagement

Everyone talks about employee engagement. We know the research and have seen the financial metrics that show the companies who get employee engagement right are more productive, profitable, and innovative. Other benefits of employee engagement include having more satisfied customers and improving the retention of top talent. Everyone knows it works.

---

14 Harvard Business School, "Toxic Workers," 2015

So now that we know the benefits of having it, let's get clear on what it is and is not.

Employee engagement is *not* about happiness and satisfaction, though being engaged will lead to happy and satisfied employees. It *is* when *employees have a deep personal relationship to the company and their fellow employees.* It *is* when *an employee goes beyond their own personal gain for the sake of the organization.* It means doing tasks, working toward goals, and going the extra mile because they want to, not simply because they have to.

So how do you attain deep emotional commitment to your company and goals, and achieve discretionary effort? There are key accelerators to employee engagement: Purpose, Clarity, Development, Recognition, and Leadership.

Purpose. *Identify and state your purpose as an organization.* What and who do you strive to be? Who are you aspiring to be? What is your value proposition and brand? Can you identify and articulate this? Be concise and clear. If you haven't fully identified your purpose, take the time to nail it down. It's connected to and drives everything you do. As your purpose comes to fruition, it should unfold into your mission, vision, values, and strategies, which all link back to how you will achieve your purpose. Your purpose is why people want to work for you, why people want to achieve greatness in your company, the reason they develop a deep emotional commitment, and a key factor to why they want to stay.

Clarity. *Get clear and be concise* with your purpose, vision, mission, strategy, and expectations. Where have you been, where are you today, and where are you going? Ask yourself these questions frequently.

Trends, methods, and tools are moving and changing at an incredible speed, and people need to know what the current line of sight is. Goals established in December are outdated by March. Are you agile enough to update and modify your goals and expectations? How does this impact your short and long-term goals?

Communicate your goals with your people (this presumes that you have asked your people for input to goals). Communicate, communicate, communicate, and then communicate some more. Most organizations believe they are communicating enough, but they aren't. Use multiple formats for communication—intranet, emails, town hall meetings, manager and team meetings, brown bag lunches, website, posters, etc.

If you asked everyone in your organization if they fully understand their responsibilities, roles, and goals, and how they are connected to the overall purpose and strategy of the organization, what would they say? Do you think they would know? Would the responses be consistent across the organization? Ask. Ask often. Ask for input and feedback often.

Development. *People want opportunities to grow, learn, and develop.* We all want advice, feedback, mentorship, and advocacy. Research has shown for many years that people leave their boss, not their organization. A manager's ability to provide multiple means of development opportunities for their people, including their own ability to develop effectively, is critical.

Do you have a mentor, advisor, and/or advocate? If not, what is your plan to get one? Within your organization, are you actively promoting mentorship? Do you have development plans for every employee that are discussed, reviewed, and updated frequently? *Today's employee wants feedback and input—often.* As the organizational direction changes, your employees' skills and objectives need to evolve as well.

One important theme of younger generations in the workforce is that they want to have an impact and move quickly. They don't look at their careers in the traditional "ladder model," they instead look at their careers in a more experiential and matrixed way. They want to learn and grow, work on projects and in teams. How many multi-functional and cross-generational project teams do you have? Does your organization support employees who rotate across jobs, functions, and geographies? Can people move quickly into expanded and advanced roles if they demonstrate outstanding results, performance, and potential?

Recognition. People *and teams* want to be recognized for their accomplishments, achievements, goals, and milestones, and for their impact and contributions. They want to be recognized financially (raises, bonuses, stock, equity, and rewards), through advancement and promotions, and through increased roles and responsibilities. Know your people, their personalities and styles, and what motivates and drives them. Depending on who they are, they will be motivated and driven by different things. Some employees want public recognition. For others, quiet, personal statements of recognition and gratitude have a much greater impact.

Leadership. The *#1 driver of employee engagement is the effectiveness of your managers in how they manage and lead*. This conclusion has been validated by more than 30 years of research. Creating a *leadership culture* and increasing the engagement of your employees can be positively impacted by providing the right learning and development programs as well as using assessments like the PI.

These key accelerators to employee engagement are critical to the overall success of your organization and how you align your organization to reach your targets for success. Create alignment. Develop your people. Have a healthy culture.

So, is leadership still important? When we look at the consequences of poor leadership, it's clear that being an effective leader is more important than ever.

In the next few chapters, I will detail the critical knowledge, skills, and behaviors that you need to be able to demonstrate to be an effective leader of today and the future.

Chapter 5: The Secret Sauce

In working with executives, I go over what I call the *secret sauce*. No matter what personality type or leadership style a person has, there is a secret sauce for being effective. This includes: passion, self-awareness, the two-sided coin of self-acceptance and self-development, handling triggers, building trust, asking for and providing feedback, and making the best use of time.

Self-Awareness

First, you have to be aware of who you are, what makes you tick, and what has shaped and formed you. That's why I started this book by sharing my own story. Research for over 30 years has shown that **self-awareness is the primary indicator to achieving high performance**. It's more than just being aware of your aspirations, motivations, and the way you handle situations and people. You must be comfortable in your own skin and not feel you need to display an image of what you want to be. In other words, being your authentic and transparent self. In order to be an authentic leader, you must understand why you are the way you are and know the experiences that have shaped you.

Some life experiences are not always positive. They may have been very dramatic, painful, and negative. Some may have been inspirational and positive. Think about your family, your schooling, and your community. All these influences shape who you are today. These experiences have had a tremendous impact on you, how you see the world, and how you respond to certain situations. These experiences can be transformational and leave an imprint on you for life. Earlier, I shared some of my own experiences. I didn't realize it at the time these things were happening, but after reflecting on them, I know they have had a significant impact on me, my values, and how I see and respond to my environment.

You react to certain situations in your life based on these powerful experiences. It's critical for a leader to pause, reflect, and discuss those experiences—what they were, why and how they influenced you, and how you react and handle challenging situations. It's important to understand how these experiences shaped you and how they influence your decisions, conflict, challenges, and stress.

It's really a combination of being situational and adaptive. You need to understand and learn how to connect with different people and different styles; how to influence people; and how to build trust and relationships with people very different from you and accept who they are. Not everyone is the same, and some people will react to situations in very different ways from you. It's important to recognize and appreciate that as you develop as a leader.

Motivations & Drives

Part of the secret sauce for leadership is accepting and understanding that people are wired differently than you. It's not just about who you are and your style. It's about what motivates and drives you. If you're a very gregarious, connecting, social person, that's not just who you are; that's what motivates and drives you. You want to connect with people. You need to have relationships with people. If you're more reserved, more introverted, or more analytical, then you're not driven by relationships. Perhaps you're driven by subject matter expertise. You need to have time to think and process and be creative.

When you're aware of your own drives, motivations and behaviors, and those of the people around you, then you can adapt. For example, let's say you have a strong, assertive, and sometimes overbearing personality. If you're dealing with a more unassuming personality who's not authoritative and who's more about harmony and collaboration, consider slowing your tempo and lowering your voice. You might ask what they think about something you said.

If you're just "doing your thing" with no awareness of the other person's motivations and drives, you most likely will be very overwhelming to that person. You probably won't get the response you were hoping for. People who are more unassuming and harmonistic are uncomfortable with conflict and will avoid it. It doesn't mean they won't have an opinion or view, but they will express it in a more passive-aggressive way. If left unaddressed, their views will begin to show up throughout an organization, versus directly with the person with whom they were engaging.

On the other hand, people who are more assertive are typically more direct and look at conflict as engaging in "healthy debate." They can appear to enjoy butting heads frequently.

Understanding people and who they are, inclusive of all their different behavioral attributes and characteristics will help you be more effective in communicating and working with people, especially when they are very different than you.

This is not about being a chameleon or manipulative. You must still be authentic and true to who you are and learn how to be adaptive or situational working with people. It's more respectful too. You're respecting the individuality of the people who work with you. But more importantly, you are finding ways to connect and be effective in working with people by adjusting your approach and style.

It's also important to take some time to self-reflect. Look back on those life experiences. Consider how you've been shaped by them, how they influence the way you are today, and how they affect your responses to certain people and situations.

Self-awareness and being aware of the experiences that have shaped you are critical. That's one aspect of it. The second is understanding your behavioral self. What is your behavioral profile? What are your strengths? What happens to you under stress and pressure? What are your derailers? How does that translate into what your natural leadership style is? Under pressure and stress, we default back to our natural selves.

To find out more about who you are, what motivates and drives you, and how you relate to others, I suggest taking a behavioral assessment like PI, which I've referenced several times. At MCG Partners, we use PI to assess behavioral styles and help people learn how to better work with people and manage themselves and others by increasing their self-awareness. We are a certified partner of PI and have represented and used PI in the marketplace for many years.

Though behavioral science began in the late 1800s, within the last 30 years it has started gaining more traction and acceptance in the business world. The shift to decisions based on "talent analytics" is becoming a major component in terms of optimizing talent for your strategic and organizational needs, and in understanding your people.

It's all about finding the connection between who people are and what motivates and drives them. This is a major ingredient of the secret sauce. As a leader, you must motivate, inspire, develop, and nurture the people in your organization. In order to do that, you have to understand what makes them tick. PI offers that insight so that as a leader, you can adapt and adjust as you work with different behavioral styles and personalities to create the optimal person, team, and organization to meet your strategic objectives.

Perception

An important aspect of self-awareness is knowing how you're perceived by others. I use a 360-degree assessment, which I referenced earlier when I had one done for myself. Confidential feedback can be a written assessment or a verbal interview with key stakeholders—subordinates, peers, boss, and other key people you work with, inside or outside of the organization.

When coaching executives, I interview the leader's key stakeholders. It's important to see how people view themselves compared to how others experience them. A 360-degree assessment often reveals a leader's lack of self-awareness and a disconnect between how they're perceived by others and how they see themselves.

For example, you may think you're an excellent collaborator and communicator, but half your stakeholders say you're not a very strong communicator and you don't work well on a team. Or the opposite may be true; you might think you're a poor leader, but others see you as excellent. This provides an understanding of how you see yourself and how others see you, which can spring ideas for how to create better alignment in those perceptions.

The 360-degree assessment provides direct feedback, giving you opportunities to see where you can improve and be more effective. It can reveal potential blind spots and help you see ways to deal with people at all levels, from your boss to your team.

Feedback

Behavioral assessments such as PIs and 360-degree assessments help give you a clearer picture of who you are, how your experiences have shaped you, and how you respond to people and situations because of those experiences. Self-awareness is an essential ingredient of the secret sauce for effective, agile leadership. Feedback and input are also critical parts of the self-awareness picture. You have to know how to effectively ask for and receive feedback and input and be equally adept at giving it.

Research continues to show that *your* ability to initiate, ask for, and be receptive to feedback on specific areas of development you are trying to address as a leader, is one of the most critical factors in being perceived by your key stakeholders as improving and progressing as a leader.

It is just as critical to give feedback as it is to receive it. Providing feedback improves performance, develops talent, aligns expectations, solves problems, holds people accountable to performance and behavior, guides promotion and pay, and boosts the bottom line.

In many organizations, feedback isn't working. Most companies try to address problems by training leaders to give feedback more effectively and more often. But improving the feedback giver's skills must go in hand with the recipient's ability to absorb what is said. The giver needs to have the courage to provide honest feedback; the recipient has to make sense of what they are hearing and decide whether or not to change or adjust. *Feedback must be delivered with courage and openly received.*

When giving feedback, ask for permission. This will signal if the recipient is ready, open, and receptive to the feedback.

Almost everyone, from new hires to C-suite veterans, struggles with receiving feedback. A critical performance review, a well-intended suggestion, or a comment that may not even be intended as feedback ("well, your presentation was certainly interesting") can spark an emotional reaction, inject tension into the relationship, and bring communication to a halt. However, the skills needed to receive feedback well are learnable. They include being able to identify and manage the emotions *triggered* (we will be reviewing triggers in a few chapters) and extracting value from criticism, even when it's poorly delivered.

I had a client that was just too direct. He often came across as abrasive; the feedback would cut right through people. His management team started to avoid or tune him out, as his style was just too harsh. I worked with him on a number of things, such as improving his self-awareness, discovering his triggers, and working on emotional intelligence and his executive presence. The technique I shared with him to give feedback more effectively was to pause, especially when under pressure or stress. Before speaking, I suggested he ask himself, *"How will my audience receive this message?"*

It may seem like a simple exercise, but it's an important one for all leaders. Does your feedback have the intent and impact of being *in the spirit of helping that person?* Are your comments going to help *your team be successful and reach their potential?* I advise clients to first ask a question, to determine how aware the person is of what you want to provide feedback on.

Feedback should be provided on a regular basis, as close to real-time as possible. As goals and objectives are in constant motion due to the ever-changing business and market climate, people need to know where they stand, and when or if their objectives have changed. Ensure you are clarifying gaps of expectations and where a person or team may be. What does success look like? Provide as many specific examples as possible. Reinforce and recognize outstanding performance. People need to understand what is considered top versus adequate performance, and they need to be engaged and motivated to continue.

Why Feedback Doesn't Register

What makes receiving feedback so hard? It strikes at the tension between two core needs—the need to learn and grow, and the need to be accepted just the way we are. As a result, even a seemingly gentle suggestion can leave you feeling angry, anxious, badly treated, or profoundly threatened. Comments like "don't take this personally" do nothing to soften the blow. Getting better at receiving feedback starts with understanding and managing the following feelings:

Message triggers are set off by the *content of the feedback.* When assessments or advice seem off-base, unhelpful, or simply untrue, you can feel angry, wronged, and exasperated.

People triggers are set off by *the person providing the feedback.* Exchanges are often tainted by what you believe about the provider ("they've got no credibility on this topic") and how you feel about your previous interactions ("after all I've done for you, I get this petty criticism?"). So you might reject coaching that you would accept on its merits if it came from someone else.

Self-Identity triggers are *all about your relationship with yourself.* Whether the feedback is right or wrong, wise or pointless, it can be devastating if it causes your sense of who you are to come undone. In such moments you'll struggle with feeling overwhelmed, defensive, or off-balance.

These responses are natural and reasonable; in some cases, they are unavoidable. The solution isn't to pretend you don't have them; it's to recognize what's happening and learn how to develop value from feedback even when it sets off one or more of your triggers. We will take a deeper look at triggers in chapter 7.

Steps to Becoming a Better Receiver of Feedback

Taking feedback well is a process of sorting and filtering. You need to understand the other person's point of view, try ideas that may at first seem a poor fit, and experiment with different ways of doing things. You also need to discard or shelve critiques that are genuinely misdirected or are not helpful right away. But it's nearly impossible to do any of those things from inside a triggered response.

Instead of being open to listen and learn, your triggers lead you to reject, counterattack, or withdraw. Work on specific techniques that can help you effectively manage and filter your triggers. Can you pause, even if for an instant, before you react verbally or through body language? Are you asking how the person you're responding to will receive your response/reaction? Will you be effective in your response/reaction? Can you wait before you respond? Do you know and are you anticipating what your triggers are and why?

The best thing you can do when receiving feedback is to listen. Don't judge, react, respond, or get defensive. If you need to ask clarifying questions, then do so.

Know your tendencies. You've been getting feedback all your life, so there are most likely patterns in how you respond. Do you defend yourself on the facts ("this is plain wrong"), argue about the method of delivery ("you're really doing this by email?"), or strike back ("you, of all people?")? Do you smile on the outside but seethe on the inside? Do you get teary or filled with righteous anger? And what role does the passage of time play? Do you tend to reject feedback in the moment, and then step back and consider it over time? Do you accept it all immediately, but later decide it's not valid? Do you agree with it intellectually but have trouble changing your behavior?

Separate the "what" from the "who." If the feedback is on-target and the advice is wise, it shouldn't matter who delivers it. But it does. You have to work to separate the message from the messenger, and then consider both.

When you set aside snap judgments and explore where feedback is coming from and where it's going, you can enter into a rich conversation.

Lean towards coaching. Some feedback is evaluative ("your rating is a 4"); some is coaching ("here's how you can improve"). Everyone needs both. Evaluations tell you where you stand, what to expect, and what is expected of you.

It's not always easy to distinguish one from the other. Is the feedback intended as a helpful suggestion, or a veiled criticism of someone's usual approach? When in doubt, people tend to assume the worst and to put even well-intentioned coaching into the evaluation bin. Feeling judged is likely to set off your identity triggers, and the resulting anxiety can drown out the opportunity to learn. Whenever possible, lean towards coaching. Work to hear feedback as potentially valuable advice from a fresh perspective rather than as an indictment of how you've done things in the past.

Press Pause. Often, it's not immediately clear whether the feedback is valid and useful. So, before you accept or reject it, do some analysis to better understand it.

When you set aside snap judgments and take time to explore where feedback is coming from and where it's going, you enter into a rich, informative conversation about perceived best practices—whether you decide to take the advice or not.

Ask for just one thing. Feedback is less likely to set off your emotional triggers if you request it, so don't wait. Find opportunities to get feedback and coaching from a variety of people/key stakeholders throughout the year. Don't ask unfocused questions like "Do you have any feedback for me?" Make the process more manageable by asking a colleague, a boss, or a direct report, "What's one thing you see me doing (or failing to do) that holds me back?"

That person may name the first behavior that comes to mind or the most important one on their list. Either way, you'll get tangible information and can flush out more specifics at your own pace.

Be as specific as you can. Research has shown the more specific you are the easier it is for the person to provide feedback and the more helpful the feedback will be. Focus on the top one or two things you are working on. For example, "I'm working on listening more and not rushing to my opinion, can you please let me know how I'm doing?" Ask for feedback after a situation where you are trying to work in a particular area.

An executive client found her 360-degree review process overwhelming and confusing. "Thirty pages of charts and graphs and trying to navigate what's most important was frustrating," she said.

Now, she taps two or three people each quarter to ask for one thing she might work on. "They don't offer the same things, but over time I hear themes, and that gives me a good sense of where my growth lies," she says. "And I have really good conversations — with my boss, with my team, even with peers where there's some friction in the relationship. They're happy to tell me one thing to change, and often they're right. It does help us work more effectively together and they seem to value that I'm receptive to and want their input."

Research has shown that leaders who clearly seek critical feedback tend to get higher performance ratings, and more importantly, are viewed as improving as leaders. Why? You are letting people know that their views and opinions matter to you; when asking for coaching you are more likely to take what is said to heart and genuinely improve; but also because when you ask for feedback, you not only find out how others see you, you also influence how they see you. Soliciting constructive input communicates humility, respect, passion for excellence, and confidence.

Test it out. After you've worked to seek and understand feedback, it may still be hard to determine which bits of advice will help you and which ones won't. I suggest designing small experiments to find out. Even though you may doubt that a suggestion will be useful, if the downside risk is small and the upside potential is large, it's worth a try. When someone gives you advice, test it out. If it works, great. If it doesn't, you can try again, tweak your approach, or decide to end the approach.

Observations or constructive criticism can be difficult to take. Even when you know that it's essential to your development and you trust that the person delivering it wants you to succeed, it can activate triggers. You might feel misjudged and sometimes threatened.

Your growth depends on your ability to pull value from criticism in spite of your natural responses, and on your willingness to seek out even more advice and coaching from bosses, peers, subordinates, friends, and mentors. They may be good or bad at providing it, or they may have little time for it—but *you are the most important factor in your own development.*

If you're determined to learn from and apply whatever feedback you receive, no one can stop you.

Passion

"People with passion can change the world
for the better. The only way to do great work
is to love what you do." – Steve Jobs

Passion is a relentless pursuit of what is important to us. **Having a passion for your work and for your life is one of the greatest joys that you can have.** It is *the* special ingredient in the secret sauce. In the increasingly challenging and competitive world we live in, if you don't have passion for what you do, how can you expect to do well, especially over a long period of time? Without that love, interest, fire, and belief, and without a personal connection, you cannot compete and be a top performer in business for the long haul.

Passion is contagious. It attracts people who are looking to find their passion and purpose and inspires people who share a common passion to take action and feel motivated.

Passion leads you to your purpose. It inspires and drives you toward your aspirations and goals, no matter how difficult they might be. It generates the enthusiasm needed to propel you through the biggest obstacles and overcome the most impossible challenges. Passion inspires loyalty, teamwork, hard work, and, eventually, success. As a manager and leader of people, you need to have passion and the desire to manage and lead. Without passion, you might be a good leader but not a great one.

I'm very fortunate as I found my true passion and purpose in life. I hope you find yours.

There are many elements to the *secret sauce* of leadership. We will continue to discover many elements throughout the book. Find elements that resonate with you. If you identified the top 10 best leaders of the world, you would find that they all have different backgrounds, education, specialties, personalities, and leadership styles. Then why are they so effective if they are so different? What are the consistent threads among them and all great leaders? Much of this will be answered in the following pages, but some of it has to do with their ability to modify their style and approach to their audience, so they can be more effective in influencing, building relationships, guiding, empowering, and motivating others. Some of it is about their innate ability to bring out the best in others, to surround themselves with the abilities and talents they don't possess. Some of it is about their ability to have a vision of what kind of organizational culture they wish to have in order to achieve their aspired state and strategic objectives, and what type of leaders they will need to make that happen.

Chapter 6: The Two-Sided Coin

While it is essential to be self-aware, to frame yourself in the knowledge of how you have been shaped by your natural self and your experiences, self-awareness alone is not enough. It can create greater clarity and open up the possibility of what I call the two-sided coin: self-acceptance and self-development.

> *"Every truth has two sides; it is as well to look at*
> *both before we commit ourselves to either." – Aesop*

Self-Acceptance

Self-acceptance means looking at yourself: every quirk, interest, and ability you either were born with, had thrust upon you, or developed yourself, and acknowledging all of it. You are who you are. Hopefully, you like this person, or at least have come to accept the good with the bad. We are all human. No one is perfect. We all have flaws and areas we can work to improve; it's important to accept and tolerate ourselves with all our flaws and areas for improvement, and celebrate all the good and beautiful things, too.

Learning this for yourself will help you show others the way. How are you going to help other people piece it together, help them improve and be more effective in their roles, and advance their careers? How are you going to help managers be effective leaders if you're struggling with self-acceptance?

We all have insecurities and doubts. Self-acceptance is not about having no insecurities. You need to choose to accept yourself, to like yourself and say, "I am who I am."

Realize that you have a certain natural style and accept that. It doesn't mean that you are not striving for improvement and to become the best you can be, but you still need to accept yourself for who you are. Self-acceptance is a critical component of the secret sauce.

I remember one particular leader who had a negative coaching experience because the coach tried to tell him to change who he was. That's just bad advice. The things that get you into trouble as a leader and as a person are always going to trip you up. Why? Because you are who you are. It's how you're wired. Certain tendencies, reactions, and preferences are learned from our environment and education, but most are built into our DNA. If you've had a very traumatic event in your life, it can affect your behavior and your identity. But that's not what we're talking about here.

It's hard to accept others and those around you if you can't accept yourself. Don't be afraid to look in the proverbial mirror to see what's inside and who you are, including the things that bother, frustrate, and annoy you.

As I've already said, there is no perfect leadership style, no model person who is destined for leadership. But also ask yourself, are you an effective leader? If not, why? If you aren't there yet, accept it. Then question it.

If you refuse to change anything about who you are right now, that could be a reason for your lack of effectiveness. Be you but *become the best version of you*. That's how one side of the coin, self-acceptance, flips to the other side: self-development.

Self-Development

You may have attended many training sessions, seminars, and speeches on self-development, on how to change what you need to change in order to become more successful. You may know exactly what you need to do next. If not, you may need to take a little more time to reflect.

Part of self-development is to be humble enough to recognize that you don't know it all; that there is something still to learn; to seek and identify your blind spots; and your development needs. This includes the things that get to you when you are under pressure and stress—that derail your effectiveness. Once you accept yourself, you have to continue to develop yourself. This lifelong journey of learning persists throughout your career, regardless of the promotions and amazing successes. If you dedicate yourself to the process, you will continue to improve, and flip the coin back and forth from self-acceptance to self-development.

Chapter 7: Triggers

You can't live in today's culture without hearing about triggers. Nearly anything anyone says to anyone else could be called a trigger. It goes back to the experiences that have shaped us, as well as who we are. Some impact us at a deep enough level that when something—even an innocent comment by a neutral person—reminds us of those events, we can react in a strong, unexpected way.

Any of us can be triggered at any time. Some people demand that others around them be careful about what they say or do in order to avoid being triggered or setting off someone else. If we could do that, it would be great. However, unless you know someone well enough to know their triggers, it's relatively impossible to avoid them. Instead of feeling responsible for avoiding everyone else's triggers or worrying about them, focus on taking ownership of your own.

The way we understand and manage our triggers is critical! It's a game-changer. Some of us do a reasonable job of masking our triggers to the outside world, but they still have a big impact on how we interact with others, and how we deal with them matters. This concept of triggers really resonates with every leader I've worked with. It's become an important ingredient in the secret sauce.

Let me walk you through my methodology and process of how you can be remarkably and noticeably better at managing your triggers and how this impacts those around you. I was my first client!

Identify Your Triggers

A trigger is anything that sets off an emotional or volatile response. In order to manage your triggers, you first need to identify them. Are there situations, people, or comments that set you off?

Maybe it's when your coworker is always late to meetings. Or it could be a person who just rubs you the wrong way. Or how about when someone says something exactly the way your mother used to say it when she was angry or disappointed with you? That's a trigger. It could be someone challenging your authority, your expertise, or your ability to do a good job.

These triggered responses are emotional surges that lead you to react in an emotional way, putting you in a position to no longer have rational or logical thought, reasoning, or decision-making. Have you ever responded to someone in a highly emotional state and felt you were reasonable, rational, balanced, and effective? If you said no, then join the rest of us mortals and realize that being triggered is a problem in all aspects of life.

The solution isn't to pretend you don't have triggers or to accept them at face value, or to believe, *it is the way it is, I can't control it.* Success is recognizing what's happening and learning how to see and take value from comments and situations, even when they set off one or more of your triggers.

Now, it's time to identify your own triggers. I use an exercise, which I will describe below, in my coaching of executives. No matter how much self-development we've done, no matter where we are in life and in our careers, or how self-aware we are, when we are under pressure and stress, we tend to go back to our natural selves.

Let's look at an example. Many leaders tend to be strong and assertive. That's a great quality for leadership, but you can overuse it. And when we overuse our strength, we overuse a behavior. We call that *derailing*. If you're very authoritative and assertive, you can derail by overusing your assertiveness and running over people, leaving a pile of bodies behind you as you stomp through those barriers and obstacles like a bull in a china shop.

You're a driver; you're a change agent. That could be a very powerful, very positive or effective aspect of leadership. But if you overuse that and make changes quickly and suddenly, people might be running around like chickens with their heads cut off, not knowing what to do and with panic setting in. That's the danger of overuse. You may be blind to the fact that you continue to go back to that tendency, or you may be aware of it. Many leaders are aware of this problem, but they don't know how to manage it. The key is to focus on triggers. Everyone I talk to, even the calmest person I've ever met in my life, understands what I'm talking about because we all have triggers. Some people will show their triggers in a very external way. They're very emotionally open that way. Some people internalize them, but the fire is still there.

As someone who also has had to learn how to deal with my own triggers, through my own journey and self-development, I came up with a methodology to address triggers and over the years have been coaching my clients to do the same.

One thing that fascinates me is how many ways we allow ourselves to be *victims of our triggers*. We know what our triggers are, but we allow ourselves to let the trigger happen, to have the reaction.

And somehow we're surprised every single time. It doesn't matter how old you are, how well you know yourself, how much life experience you've had. We allow the trigger to affect us as though we're just helpless to stop it. Then we feel bad. Then we have to apologize for the damage we caused to the relationship, whether it happened with a friend, a family member, or someone at work. Wouldn't it be nice if you were no longer a victim of your triggers? Let's talk about a process to get to that point.

Know and Manage Your Triggers

Get your notebook and a pen. You're going to need three columns. In the first column, write out your triggers. In the second column, write why they are a trigger. What is it about that particular thought, or phrase, or situation that causes you to react?

If you're not sure what being triggered looks like for you, think about what happens when you react emotionally. Just as there are many different triggers, there are different reactions. Perhaps you become very abrupt or abrasive, cut people off, start yelling, slam a door, hang up on someone, send a nasty email, walk out of a room, or shut down. Or, maybe you sit there and do nothing at the time, but later go around telling everybody how awful the person is who triggered you. There are many different avenues of how you can demonstrate being triggered—aggressive, passive-aggressive, etc. Think through what happens, what causes it, and why.

When you're triggered, you're reactive. You're creating a reaction based upon something that's tweaking you emotionally. Again, some of us internalize it, some of us externalize it. No matter how you express it, the fact is that when you're having that strong emotional reaction, you can't think and act rationally and logically.

We'd like to think we can. We've all tried and failed miserably. I'm talking about CEOs of Fortune 500 companies, nonprofit directors, mid-level managers—all different ages, different genders, from different cultures across the globe. We all experience triggers. We all handle them differently. But unfortunately, if we don't manage them effectively, they have a negative effect. It's like someone who's had too much to drink and thinks they can still have an intelligent conversation or drive effectively.

So, how do we change that? How do we react differently? You can't think through it in the moment, so you have to think through it before it happens. That's what this next step of the exercise is for.

After you've written out your triggers and why they exist, the third step is the key. What are you going to do differently? Think through it now, before you're feeling the reaction. Try to *visualize* the scenario of where you are and what is triggering you, and how you will now respond in a more effective way.

The whole concept of visualization started with athletes. This works for runners, Olympic athletes, any sport really, and it works for actors and actresses too. Visualization is as important as physical practice. Athletes who visualize themselves with the ability to perform or achieve or execute in their particular sport are often able to achieve at higher levels. If you've made the shot 1,000 times sitting at your desk while you're solving that problem, you're more likely to make it on the court.

Visualization is an effective tool as you make improvements in many areas of life, including, managing triggers. Take some time to pause and reflect. Start visualizing your triggers one at a time. What is your typical response? Now, what are you going to do differently?

Even if you've had the same triggers and the same responses for as long as you can remember, now is as good of a time as ever to make a decision. Stop being a victim now. **Take *ownership* of your triggers and stop being a victim of them**. Now that you know what they are and you can see them coming, take responsibility for changing your behavior.

When you begin to feel a trigger—you'll know when it's coming on— pause. Take a breath. Take a break. Go for a walk outside. It's the proverbial count to ten. In other words, don't send that email, don't respond, and don't open your mouth. Take a breath and smile. Ah yes, I said smile, maybe even a small laugh. *There is nothing better to diffuse yourself, an escalation, or a conflict than a sincere smile or laugh.* Think of something positive or consider that maybe you are being silly, trivial, or obnoxious and that it's time to change the current mood.

Something I've used to de-escalate myself and to diffuse my triggers is a line from a well-known movie: "He's an angry Elf." It works for me. It makes me smile and laugh. Use something that works for you! Keep telling yourself this, and don't be a victim of your trigger. Own it! Take ownership and responsibility of how you will respond.

Part of the nature of triggers is that they catch you off guard. You're still occasionally going to be surprised. Now, your first reaction needs to be pause, stop, and do nothing. Silence. I don't care who you are, this works. If you are a person who is very emotional or intense, it may be a struggle at first. It may even be a struggle every time. But you've got to pause before you react. Your pause might look different depending on how you're being triggered. That's why you need to write them out in a list.

You know what the triggers are and why they trigger you. In that third column, write down the best way you can think of to handle each of your triggers. Then practice. Visualize yourself walking through a situation where a particular trigger is likely to happen. Imagine yourself dealing with it like a rational human. Take the time you need to learn how to manage each of them.

Pay attention to your body language. It's often not what you say and how you say it, even though we all know how damaging that can be; it's often about your facial expression, your overall body language—arms crossed, leaning across the table, fingers or feet pattering. No one will ever want me as a poker-playing partner. I have a hard time controlling the emotions on my face, but we all must try, and be more facially measured. You get the idea. As mentioned earlier, how are you going to diffuse yourself and the situation? Smile, laugh (appropriately, not like a wild hyena), or even change the conversation? Observe the person or group and how they're doing. What are their challenges at the moment? How can you help them? Shifting a conversation, without ignoring the person or their issues, can also be very effective.

Now, just because you've done the exercise and know what you need to do, what behavioral modification you need to make, what adjustments you need to make, or how to adapt situationally, doesn't mean you're always going to do it right. It takes more than flipping a switch. Modification and change are very, very hard. It's a process. It takes incremental steps, practice, and time.

Let's go back to physical practice to illustrate this. It's like the person who wants to go to the gym and see physical improvement. They may want to lose weight, gain muscle, or increase endurance —just get in better shape. But they want to see immediate results. They want to put in a couple of sessions and look like a fitness model or world-class athlete or lose a few pounds. Unfortunately, for the majority of people, if they don't get that instant gratification, change, or improvement, they're disappointed. They quit.

We live in a world of instant gratification, but behavior improvement and physical improvement don't work that way. You want to improve your physical body, lose weight, be stronger, or have better endurance? You need to commit, and you've got to work hard on it. It's going to take a couple of months to start seeing improvement. With behavior modification changes, it's no different. You've got to work on it. You have to put in the hours and the effort, and it can take a lot of time before you notice a difference.

You're human. You will make mistakes and someday you will catch yourself in the middle of a reaction. As soon as you realize you're doing it, stop. You may have done some damage, but you have to start somewhere.

You start by paying attention to triggers and deciding how you're going to manage them differently. You may have to be creative. The answer might not come right away. This is hard work. You've got to commit. You have to want to get better at this.

We all know this intellectually, but it doesn't always translate to actual reality. You could be great with people 99% of the time, and then one of your triggers pops up. It could be that really bad email. You know the kind. Capital letters and exclamation points. It could arrive at a moment when you're already frustrated or tired. The trigger hits, and you lose it.

Are you a failure? Has that undermined your entire leadership career? No, because you've been working on it, and the other 99 times out of 100, you get it right. But unfortunately, people don't remember the 99 times you got it right; they remember the triggered reaction.

Triggers are often seen as an issue that mainly affects explosive, emotional people, but that's not the case. Maybe you are a more relaxed, easygoing, and quiet person; more passive-aggressive than emotional. But you can do just as much damage when you're triggered. Everyone is different, and you have to learn to manage your own triggers in a way that works for you. Managing triggers is a critical component of being effective.

There are worst-case scenarios. Someone could just have a blow-up that goes through the company and changes everything; now everyone is talking about what happened. That's a highly observable trigger, and it can be extremely damaging. Whether you see a lot of emotion or none at all, it's very possible for a triggered person to do extensive damage. That is what we all want to avoid.

But what if you didn't mean to? What if you made a mistake and it all blew up? I always talk about intent versus impact. We may have the best intentions in the world, but if your impact is negative, again, whether it's because you're being too assertive or because you're being too critical, or because you're being passive-aggressive and damaging in other ways, your impact can be worse than what you intend. In those situations, people tend to say, "well, I tried to handle it the best I could."

You've got to accept ownership. You may have the best intentions in the world, but what's the impact you're having? There are some people who are going to get to you, push your buttons either maliciously or unintentionally. Don't take the bait. You need to understand what bothers you and how to manage the triggers. It's about understanding what triggers you so that you're not only avoiding new and future triggers, but you're also taking ownership of how you react.

Managing your triggers effectively by being more measured doesn't mean that you need to be robotic or manipulative. You want to be authentic and true to yourself and effective in how you interact and influence others, and your ability to manage conflict, pressure, and stress, while building strong and trusting relationships.

After some practice, you will be able to identify when a trigger is coming. Write down how you know you're being triggered, and how to recognize it BEFORE the reaction.

No matter how small, large, or inconsequential you think your reaction to a trigger may have been, always apologize. Wait until you are calm, and the situation has calmed down, but apologize. Be sincere, earnest, and humble. Ask for feedback from a trusted colleague about your progress. Capture feedback on successes as well as failures to have positive insights to build on.

Being Right Is Irrelevant

One thing you can watch for, and hopefully avoid, is the *volcano effect*. This can happen when someone hasn't learned to manage their triggers well. They don't react to them in the moment, but instead they internalize and let them heat up over time. The pressure builds until anything, even something insignificant, causes an eruption. If you're on the receiving end, you may be blown away, thinking "What happened? Maybe we didn't have the best interaction, but surely it wasn't that bad!"

Avoid becoming a volcano by managing your triggers and try to deal with other people in healthy ways before you explode. Don't let things build up over time; address your issue or frustration when it happens.

One thing I often tell clients is, *"Being right is irrelevant."* Many leaders have a strong value system they believe in or very strong beliefs and opinions. With that comes a need to be right. They don't like to be questioned, challenged, or contradicted because it feels like an attack on their identity, views, beliefs, expertise, or experience. They have a need to prove or demonstrate that they are right. There is a kind of stubborn insistence here: "Of course I'm right. Don't question me!" or, "I'm the leader, I'm in charge, the decision is mine!"

You may know how this feels. And in these situations, you may be right. Not always, but often. Even if you're right, clinging to your need to prove it may undermine your leadership. Think again about *intent versus impact*. Sometimes being right is irrelevant. Recall the expression, "you may win the battle but lose the war." There may be times when proving you're right costs more in the long run, in terms of damaging your relationships and the effectiveness of your team.

There is a terrific expression about *intellectual humility* — it's about recognizing that what you believe in might in fact be wrong. It's not about being a pushover; it's not about lacking confidence, or self-esteem. *It's about being open to learning from the experience of others and to hear opposing views.*

Take a moment to let go of your leadership ego. Hear people out. Try to understand an issue from someone else's perspective. Ask honest, non-leading questions. Ensure active listening to gain alignment and understanding. Maybe you're not as right as you thought you were. Even if you are, taking the time to listen goes a long way. Better to sacrifice the small win of the moment than lose the victory of future success.

Learn to own your triggers and you'll keep them from owning you. Demonstrating greater emotional control and consistency will have a dramatic impact on your ability as a manager and leader to develop trust and create a safe environment.

Chapter 8: Trust - Your Key to Success

The next ingredient in the secret sauce of leadership effectiveness is trust. Leadership thrives in the midst of trusting relationships. If you don't establish trust with people, you're not going to have a strong enough relationship to engage them and to lead them.

Inclusive of your personality type, whether or not you're a "people person," if you don't form relationships with people there's no level of trust. If people don't trust you, how are you going to be effective? How can you effectively deal with or address conflict? Without trust, it's difficult to deal with the elephant in the room or the root cause of the conflict. Whether you're working with a peer, a boss, subordinate, or a key person in the organization, or someone externally, you've got to establish trust. You've got to invest in the relationship.

Relationships that Work

Trust is a cornerstone of leadership. There are some leaders who think it's not really that relevant. They're wrong. If people don't trust you, your intentions, or your vision, they will not follow you. If they feel you have an agenda, are being political, or are self-focused, you will never truly be effective as a leader. You may have some success, but at some point, it will impact your effectiveness. You need to have a foundation of trust in order to have effective relationships. It doesn't mean you're going to be best friends with everybody. It doesn't mean you're going to like everybody, or that everyone's going to like you. It's about gaining and giving respect. It's building credibility. It's finding common ground. It's recognizing that trust, respect, and relationships are bidirectional: you trusting your people, and your people trusting you.

What do you really need to know about a person to establish trust?

Who they are. What is their persona? What motivates and drives them? Do you really know who that person is and what makes them tick? Do you know their background and experiences of what led them to where they are today? You don't need to know everything about that person, but you do need to know who they are. Some can establish a connection and build relationships quickly; others are more skeptical or just take longer to build relationships. It's important to understand the differences.

What is important to them. Why do they do what they do professionally? Why do they work where they work? What gets them excited to start each day? What keeps them awake at night? What is important to them? What are their aspirations in life? If you can't answer these questions, and they don't know this about you, it will be very difficult to establish a healthy professional relationship and to establish trust.

Who they are outside of work. You don't need to be their best friend, but you do need to know about their immediate family, including names, where they're from, and their interests and hobbies. There may be an opportunity to find a *shared experience*—something you both have a similar interest in, passion for, or experience with.

Show you care. Relationships are about checking in and having conversations. Show sincere interest in someone as a person, not just their role, tasks, and responsibilities. When's the last time you just checked in without a work agenda? Show you care.

I had a client with whom I was struggling to connect. I was unsure if things would work out. It was the first time in my career that

I'd experienced this. He didn't seem like he wanted to be in a coaching program, he was concise and short in his responses, and he was just not letting me in.

We would typically meet in a conference room. Then it hit me: I needed to meet him at his office so I could learn something about him—figure out a way to connect with him and maybe find a shared experience with him. It would be my last-ditch effort. When we met in his office, I spotted a few photos. I asked about them, and he reacted mildly positively, speaking briefly about his family. But his demeanor didn't change much.

Then, I asked him about an unusual framed image; something you wouldn't typically see hanging in an office. It was a framed poster from the 1989 Aerosmith World Concert Tour. He immediately brightened up, his eyes got larger, and he excitedly began to tell me his lifelong passion for Aerosmith. He said he was one of their biggest fans and had traveled around the world to see them. He even had backstage passes to meet the band, and proudly reported that the band knew him by his name. I asked him a few questions and we spoke about it for 30 minutes. I had struck gold. It completely changed the dynamic of our relationship, as we found something that he was passionate about and that allowed us to connect and build a strong relationship.

Below is a personality grid to help you better understand different behavioral attributes and characteristics, and how people with different styles and behaviors see others who are similar and those who are different. This will help you recognize these similarities and differences, and provide you with insights on how to modify your approaches so you can be more effective with people:

The Personality Grid:
Differences in Personalities and How We Respond

DOMINANCE – LOW

If your dominance is LOW, your typical behaviors:	If your dominance is LOW, what do you need?
• Cooperative	• Encouragement
• Accepting of company policies	• Reassurance
• Accommodating	• Harmony
• Pleasing	• Understanding
• Harmony-seeking	• Team recognition
• Collaborative	• Freedom from individual competition
• Obliging	• Opportunities to collaborate

DOMINANCE – HIGH

If your dominance is HIGH, your typical behaviors:	If your dominance in HIGH, what do you need?
• Independent	• Independence
• Assertive	• Control of own activities
• Self-confident	• To be challenged
• Venturesome	• Understanding of the big picture
• Competitive	• Autonomy in problem solving
• Comfortable with conflict	• Individual recognition
• Autonomous	• Opportunities to work with others

How am I Perceived by Others?

	Someone who is HIGH in Dominance might perceive this behavior as:	Someone who is LOW in Dominance may view this behavior as:
If You are HIGH in Dominance	• Independent • Decisive • Takes Ownership • Confident • Authoritative	• Individualistic • Pushy • Uncompromising • Aggressive • Dominating
If You are LOW in Dominance	• Not sure of yourself • Passive-aggressive • Too agreeable • Struggles to make tough decisions	• Cooperative • Team Oriented • Collaborative • Unassuming

The Personality Grid:
Differences in Personalities and How We Respond

EXTROVERSION – LOW

If your extroversion is LOW, your typical behaviors:	If your extroversion is LOW, what do you need?
• Introspective	• Opportunities to reflect
• Matter-of-fact	• Room for introspection
• Analytical	• Freedom from office politics
• Imaginative	• Private recognition
• Reflective	• Privacy
• Pensive	• Time to trust others
	• Opportunities to work with facts

EXTROVERSION – HIGH

If your extroversion is HIGH, your typical behaviors	If your extroversion is HIGH, what do you need?
• Outgoing	• Opportunities to interact
• People Oriented	• Social acceptance
• Persuasive	• Opportunities to influence
• Stimulating	• Public recognition
• Enthusiastic	• Connection with others
• Empathetic	• Visible signs of accomplishments
• Sociable	• Opportunities to work with others

How am I Perceived by Others?

	Someone who is HIGH in Extroversion may see you as:	Someone who is LOW in Extroversion might perceive your behavior as:
If You are HIGH in Extroversion	• Outgoing • Enthusiastic • Stimulating • Empathetic	• Superficial • Egotistical • Loud/Overly Talkative • Center of Attention
If You are LOW in Extroversion	• Private • Quiet • Awkward • Anti-social/Unfriendly	• Reflective • Takes things seriously • Sincere • Focused

The Personality Grid:
Differences in Personalities and How We Respond

PATIENCE - LOW

If your patience is low, your typical behaviors:	If your patience is low, what do you need?
• Intense	• Variety, change
• Restless	• Opportunities to work at a faster than average pace
• High strung	• Mobility
• Driving	• Freedom of repetition
• Impatient	• Opportunities to handle multiple priorities
• Rushed	• Freedom from routine
• Fast-paced	

PATIENCE - HIGH

If your patience is high, your typical behaviors:	If your patience is high, what do you need?
• Agreeable	• Long term affiliation
• Patient	• Ability to work at a steady pace
• Stable	• Familiar surroundings
• Calm	• Stable work environment
• Deliberate	• Freedom from changing priorities
• Comfortable with the familiar	• Supportive work team
• Steady	• Recognition for loyalty

How am I Perceived by Others?

	Someone who is HIGH in Patience may view you as:	Someone who is LOW in Patience might interpret your behavior as:
If You are HIGH in Patience	• Calm • Dependable • Reliable • Easy-going	• Struggles with change • Struggles to juggle multiple priorities • Struggles to keep up • Too methodical
If You are LOW in Patience	• Acts too quickly • Too rushed • Unfocused • Intense	• Will get it done • Results-oriented • Change is to improve • Good multi-tasker

The Personality Grid:
Differences in Personalities and How We Respond

FORMALITY - LOW

If your formality is LOW, your typical behaviors:	If your patience is LOW, what do you need?
• Informal	• Freedom from rigid structure
• Tolerant of uncertainty	• Freedom of expression
• Flexible	• Opportunities to delegate details
• Spontaneous	• Freedom from rules and controls
• Non-conforming	• Flexibility
• Casual	• Informality
• Adaptable	• Opportunities to be spontaneous

FORMALITY - HIGH

If your formality is HIGH, your typical behaviors:	If your formality is HIGH, what do you need?
• Serious	• Understanding of rules and regulations
• Diligent	• Specific knowledge of the job
• Reserved	• Freedom from risk of error
• Thorough	• Time to regain expertise
• Precise	• Recognition for depth of knowledge
• Organized	• Clarity of expectations
• Cautious	• Certainty

How am I Perceived by Others?

	Someone who is HIGH in Formality may view you as:	Someone who is LOW in Formality may see you as:
If you are HIGH in Formality	• Thorough • Organized • Structured • Detailed	• Risk adverse • Skeptical • Too structured • Perfectionist
If you are LOW in Formality	• Disorganized • Inaccurate • Too risky • Too casual • Shoots from the hip	• Flexible • Adaptable • Willing to take risk • Relaxed • Non-conforming

Source: The Predictive Index, MCG Partners

Communication That Works

You cannot become a great leader without being a great communicator. We were trained in school to focus on grammar, vocabulary, enunciation, and delivery. In other words, we were taught to focus on ourselves versus others.

It comes as no great surprise that most leaders spend the majority of their time in some type of interpersonal situation. It's also no great shock that a large number of organizational problems are the result of poor communication. Effective communication is an essential component of professional success, whether it is at the interpersonal, intergroup, intra-group, organizational, or external level.

Skills acquired and knowledge gained are only valuable to the extent that they can be practically applied. The #1 thing great communicators have in common is a heightened sense of situational and contextual awareness.

The best communicators are great *listeners* and are astute in their observations. Great communicators are skilled at reading a person or group by sensing the moods, dynamics, attitudes, values, and concerns of the people around them. Not only do they read the environment well, but they also possess the uncanny ability to adapt their message to the situation without missing a beat. The message is not about the messenger. It is about meeting the needs and expectations of those with whom you're communicating.

Build Relationships. There is great truth in the saying, "People don't care how much you know until they know how much you care." Traditional business theory tells us to stay at arm's length; don't get too close. In reality, you should do this only if you want to remain in the dark, receiving only highly sanitized versions of the truth. If you don't develop meaningful relationships with people, you'll never know what's really on their minds until it's too late to do anything about it.

Listen. Great leaders know when to dial it up, dial it down, and dial it off. Constantly repeating your message will not have the same result as engaging in meaningful conversation. The greatest communication takes place within a two-way conversation, not through a lecture or monologue. When you begin to understand that knowledge is not gained by moving your lips, but rather by removing your earwax, you have taken the first step to becoming a skilled communicator. I will go over the approach that will literally change your life if you do it effectively. It's in chapter 11, *The Art of Asking Questions*.

Get Specific. Specificity is better than ambiguity. Learn to communicate with clarity. Simple and concise is always better than complicated and confusing. Don't try to impress someone with how smart you are by using big, complicated words and descriptions. Time has never been a more precious commodity. It is critical to know how to cut to the chase and hit the high points, and to expect the same from others. Understand the value of brevity and clarity or people will tune you out long before you get to your point.

Know Your Stuff. Develop a command over your subject matter. If you don't possess subject matter expertise, few people will give you the time of day. Most successful people have little interest in listening to individuals who can't add value to a situation or topic but still force themselves into a conversation just to hear their own voice.

The "fake it until you make it" days have long since passed, and "fast and slick" sounds too good to be true. Although the delivery of your message is important, the content of your message is what truly matters. Good communicators address both the "what" and "how" aspects of messaging so they don't become the smooth talker who leaves people with the impression of form over substance. Prepare, prepare, and prepare for your communications. Know what you plan to say but be flexible enough to respond to your audience.

Be Open-Minded. The rigidity of a closed mind greatly limits new opportunities. People take their game to a whole new level when they seek out those who hold different and opposing opinions with the goal of understanding what they're thinking rather than changing their minds. *Don't be fearful of opposing views*; be genuinely curious and interested. Create a dialogue with those who confront, challenge, and stretch you. Be willing to listen, discuss, and learn with an open mind.

Read. Take a moment and reflect back on any great leader that comes to mind. You'll find they are very adept at reading between the lines. They have the uncanny ability to understand what is not said. They know how to observe.

Being a leader should not be viewed as a license to increase the volume of rhetoric. In this age of instant communication, everyone seems to be in such a rush to say what's on their minds that they fail to realize what can be gained from the minds of others. Keep your eyes and ears open and your mouth shut, and you'll be amazed at how you will raise your level of organizational awareness.

Be Selective About Your Communications. Think about the piece of information or feedback you need to deliver. Then consider the best format in which to share it. Should you speak in person, schedule a phone call or videoconference, or send an email or send a text? This is one of the biggest issues in the workplace today. How people communicate through email or text or social media versus picking up the phone or walking into someone's office or cubicle is directly connected to what you need to say. Consider how the recipient prefers to communicate but also what will be the most effective, so your opinion, response, or issue isn't misunderstood.

Be aware that tone and intent can be easily misconstrued in an email or text. Email or text is effective for stating facts and providing information and updates. When email or text is used to debate, provide opinions and feedback, or to try to influence or persuade, bad things happen. People begin to misunderstand, sensitivities are raised, escalation between parties intensifies, people are drawn into the conflict unnecessarily, and it's all on record.

Too much time, energy, and stress are wasted due to ineffectively using email or text. When in doubt of how your audience may interpret your intent, pick up the phone or visit them.

Focus on Leave-Behinds, not Take-Aways. The best communicators are not only skilled at learning and gathering information while communicating, but they are also adept at transferring ideas, aligning expectations, inspiring action, and spreading their vision. The key is to approach each interaction with a servant's heart. When you truly focus on contributing more than receiving, you will accomplish the goal. Although this may seem counterintuitive, intensely focusing on others' wants, needs, and desires will teach you far more than you'd ever learn by focusing on your agenda.

Replace Ego with Empathy. When candor is communicated with empathy and care instead of arrogance, overstated pride, or an inflated ego, good things begin to happen. Be authentic, transparent, and true to yourself and others. Be humble, accept yourself and others. You'll find this transforms anger into respect and doubt into trust.

Speak to Groups as Individuals. Leaders don't always have the luxury of speaking to individuals in an intimate setting. Great communicators can tailor a message to speak with 10 people in a conference room or 10,000 people in an auditorium and leave everyone with the feeling that they were spoken to directly. Knowing how to work a room and establish credibility, trust, and rapport are keys to successful interactions.

Tell a Story. Provide context to your message or your point of view by illustrating it with a story. Stories provide context and they are powerful in having your audience connect with you and what you are trying to convey. They can paint a visual image with which people can connect.

Change the Message If Necessary. Know how to prevent a message from going bad, and what to do when it does. Be prepared and develop a contingency plan. Keep in mind: to have successful interactions, your objective and your audience must be in alignment. If your expertise, empathy, and clarity don't have the desired effect, you still need to make an impact by adjusting on the fly. Use great questions, humor, stories, analogies, relevant data—and where appropriate—bold statements, to develop the confidence and trust needed for people to want to engage. While it is sometimes necessary, this tactic should be reserved as a last resort.

Don't assume someone is ready to have a particular conversation with you just because you're ready to have it with them. Spending time paving the way for a productive conversation is far better than going into it on the fly.

Don't assume anyone knows where you're coming from. If you fail to justify your message with knowledge, business logic, reason, and empathy, you will find that the message will often fall on deaf ears, needing reinforcement or clarification afterward.

When you have a message to communicate, make sure the message is transparent, true, correct, well-reasoned, and validated by solid logic that is specific, consistent, clear, and accurate. Be comfortable and authentic in having difficult discussions when necessary. Spending a little extra time on the front end will likely save you from considerable aggravation and damage control on the back end. Communication is not about you, your opinions, your positions, or your circumstances. It's about helping others by meeting their needs, understanding their concerns, and adding value to their world.

People don't open up to those they don't trust. When people sense a person is worthy of their trust, they will invest time and take risks in ways they wouldn't if that person or leader had a reputation built upon poor character, a lack of integrity, or mistrust. While you can demand trust, going that route doesn't work. Trust is created by earning it. Earn it by developing strong relationships, being an effective communicator, and demonstrating the appropriate actions, thoughts, and decisions. Keep in mind that people will forgive many things where trust exists but will rarely forgive where trust is absent.

Chapter 9: Time - Our Most Precious Gift

The next ingredient of the secret sauce is time. Time is without a doubt one of the most important things you have and can give.

There is always an infinite amount of work. If you have a hard time saying no, or a hard time prioritizing your tasks, you'll drown. Working longer hours is not the answer. Your time is your most valuable resource. You can't make more. You can't pause it. You can only allocate it.

What can you take out of your schedule, your day, or your week? Do you have time for reflection and development? Time to think, plan, and be strategic? Time for your family and friends? If you don't, change where you spend your time and start now. Don't look back on a life of regret. Take control and charge of your time.

Don't just give people your time, give them your attention. When you engage in conversations with people, do you listen? Some people are totally focused on what they want to say. They're experts, they want to be in charge, and they want to be right. But as we've already reviewed, many of those things are not as important as we want to believe they are.

Leadership is about listening and asking questions. If you're talking more than 30% of the time during a conversation, you're not going to be an effective leader. A leader facilitates dialogue. A leader teaches by asking questions that lead people down a path, not by telling them what to do or where to go. That's what managers do: listen, be focused, be present, and truly give people both your time and attention. That's leadership.

We will discuss in the next chapter the critical importance of where you spend your time and how you utilize it.

Being Present

There are so many distractions in the work environment these days: phones, computers, emails, schedules, and to-do lists. There's so much going on and so much to do. You can feel being pulled in many directions at once, but when you're in front of people, give them your attention. This could be in a meeting or a one-on-one conversation. If you're with someone, be *present*.

Can you slow yourself down? Can you quiet your mind, focus, be present, and listen to the people you're talking to? When you talk to someone, do you treat them like the most important person in that room?

Earlier in my career, I worked with an executive who I will never forget. One of his biggest "superpowers" was his ability to focus on the person with whom he was interacting. I experienced this when we spoke. He always made you feel that you were the most important person with whom he could be. I haven't forgotten how powerful that feeling can be.

Think about experiences you've had with people who do that well. Even if you never see that person again, you feel connected in a very unique way. Some people do it naturally, but anyone can learn how. Anyone can do it authentically if you truly care; if you understand the power and the impact of presence.

Everyone wants that kind of attention. We all want to feel important and valued, that our time and attention are respected. It's critical. Think of how you feel when the opposite happens. When you walk into a meeting, or even a restaurant or social event, and you're ignored, how do you feel? How does that set the tone for the experience?

It's usually not intentional. Sometimes we're distracted or focused on someone or something else. Sometimes people are in the middle of something else and they can't shift or pivot quickly. According to recent research, *it takes less than three seconds to make a first impression* based on your appearance, facial expressions, and level of attention. **What do you want that first impression to say about you?** Do you want it to say that you're present in the moment, or that you're distracted by other things that you deem more important?

Most people are willing to wait a few moments while you wrap up a previous task or conversation. Once you shift your focus, give people your full attention. Shut your brain off from whatever you were focused on before. *Send the message that the person you're talking to is the most important person in the room right now.* That is key.

We have a focus problem in the world we live in right now. There are distractions everywhere, and it can be easy to lose that laser focus. But if you want to be an effective leader, you've got to learn how to shut distractions down and really be present.

You don't have to be a "people person." You could be one of the most introverted people in the world and still be great at being present. I met a Buddhist monk once who barely talked, but when I spoke to him, he was fully there, as if there was no one else there with us. He wasn't thinking about anything else; he was 100% with me.

This is essential for leaders. You've probably heard the expression, "the further you move up into the organization, the more you're under the microscope." People are watching. What will they see from you? Will you give them your time? That is truly a powerful gift.

Listening

What is one of the best ways to assure people of your presence in a conversation? By listening to them. Great leaders know how to listen. Most people don't talk just because they like to hear the sound of their own voice. They want to know you hear them and value what they have to say.

Are you a good listener? If you really want to know, ask someone close to you who will answer honestly. Chances are even if you are a good listener most of the time, you still have room to improve. Good listeners are present, not distracted. They make eye contact, nod, and interact. They are active listeners, asking clarifying questions and restating to you what they heard so they can interpret it correctly. They are open to suggestions, not defensive. Remember, being right is irrelevant.

Learning

If you are listening, you are learning. Some people might argue that being curious is a natural characteristic, but as a leader you really need to be committed to learning. You need to be open-minded, and not just to your boss, but to your customers, your peers, your subordinates, and the marketplace. This is a critical component of leading. You want to avoid thinking you've "arrived."

We'll look later in more depth at this "I've arrived" idea, but for now it's important to understand that you've not yet learned everything you need to learn. Once you feel you're one of the experts in the world, the problem is that you're no longer open to learning. You're not open to input and feedback. You stop being curious.

Avoid the temptation to think that once you've reached the pinnacle of your career, you don't need to learn anymore. You're basically telling everybody that you're done. And then, frankly, you become a liability to yourself. Some people are so full of their own expertise. I've been there; I've done that. Ironically, when you stop listening and stop learning, no one listens to you.

Reverse Mentorship

One of the things we talk about with leaders today is reverse mentorship. The traditional mentorship model is senior people with experience who are mentoring junior people.

Hopefully, you've been fortunate to have had mentors in your life.

Reverse mentorship is exactly what it sounds like: a senior-level person being mentored by a more junior person. It really can be about anything. A great example is a client who was promoted to running a multibillion-dollar technology business. The problem was that he knew nothing about its products and technology. I asked him if he had an up-and-coming, high-potential technical engineer that could spend time with him to teach him about the technology. He had someone who fit that description, so they met once a week for a number of weeks. It accelerated this executive's ability to understand the business, help shape new strategies and ventures, and interact effectively with clients. It also provided the junior some important professional visibility to senior management, along with expanded experiences. That's how reverse mentorship works.

Who are your mentors? Who are your advocates? Who are your allies? You can't succeed as a leader or in life without having them. To keep these people around, you have to be willing to learn and to receive feedback and input, even when it's something you don't want to hear.

Courage

Leaders need the courage to deal with conflict, have difficult conversations, take calculated risks, and be decisive. Difficult situations come up at work, and how you as a leader handle those situations can have a big impact on your culture. Have the courage to act.

Courageous dialogue. Resolving conflict requires courage. When leaders deal with conflict in a weak, timid, passive way, or avoid it completely, it can quickly escalate into a number of problematic trends, including a toxic work environment. It can cause your best people to become disengaged or leave, morale and overall performance to suffer, and your culture to dissipate. Why? Your people want to see issues, non-performance, or bad behavior addressed, even when it's very difficult and involves a top performer or long-term employee. Good leaders deal with conflict and difficult situations in an appropriate way before they grow. This requires what I call *courageous dialogue.*

Courageous dialogue is necessary when you have to give constructive/negative feedback or resolve conflict. Why do these conversations require courage? Because they are difficult. The tendency is to ignore the problem and hope it will go away. I've worked with a lot of leaders who are wired like this. They struggle with giving bad feedback. They struggle with conflicts. It often feels highly uncomfortable. Whether the conflict is between other people, or between you and another person, be brave enough to have the conversation. Otherwise, you could create a dangerous buildup that leads to the *volcano effect* and which could impair the *safe environment* you have created.

This is becoming a major problem in organizations and leadership teams right now. We want everyone to be tolerant. We don't want to step on any eggshells or put ourselves into awkward situations and be accused of doing something wrong or bad. Managers and organizations are afraid of upsetting people and of making people uncomfortable.

In these situations, it's wise to exercise caution. But the downside of that is people are not dealing with "the elephant in the room." That "room" could be the whole leadership team, or any area where conflict or discomfort exists.

Unfortunately, we're not addressing the real issues because we're afraid of conflict, stepping on someone's toes, triggers, and the volcano. With everyone stepping around the difficult conversations or using political speak to diffuse them, they're not having the important and courageous dialogue.

As a result, the volcano grows, or the elephants never go away. It can then ripple through the entire organization. Employees feel anxious, maybe even lose sleep over it, and stop functioning well at work. Engagement suffers, as well as performance. Leaders can stop all that before it starts by being willing to have difficult conversations when necessary.

You can have courageous dialogue and difficult conversations while being respectful, empathic, calm, and non-triggered. It's critical that you are.

Courageous decision-making. In addition to resolving conflict, courage is also required in making tough and bold decisions.

Agile Leaders know their organizations must evolve and grow. Don't rest on your laurels, your reputation, or the legacy of your brand. "This is how we've always done it" is the kiss of death in today's business world. Have the courage to look into the future and make the decisions today that will propel your organization into that future in a position of strength. Challenge the status quo and give permission for others to do the same. Allow mistakes and failure, within reason. Our greatest advancements have been due to those who had the courage to see the future, overcome many failures, learn, adjust, be resilient and determined, and then deliver.

Don't be the company that refused to change with the times, and as a result ceased to exist. Blockbuster Video is a famous example. Netflix offered to sell its service to Blockbuster in 2000, but Blockbuster refused. Now Netflix is a major media company worth billions of dollars, and Blockbuster is gone. Yahoo! had opportunities to buy both Facebook and Google. Lack of vision leads to hesitation toward risk.

Caution is wise, but knowing when to make a courageous decision, to challenge the status quo, to be willing to expand or change your vision, and your strategy is agile leadership.

Chapter 10: The Leadership Shift

A New Formula for Success

Once you've mastered *the secret sauce*, you gain a competitive advantage. As you advance your career, especially in every level of management you will take on, you will have to make shifts in your mindset, schedule, approach, and work habits.

If you were elevated into a higher management role because of the success at your job and the value you provide to your company, I have good news and bad news for you. The good news is you have unlocked some of the secrets of success. Congratulations! Now for the bad news: The winning formula that got you to where you are in your career today will most likely not carry you into success tomorrow.

Early in your career, you spend most of your time developing your expertise, demonstrating a high level of performance, and then moving into management. As previously mentioned in chapter 3, managing is teaching people what to do. It's holding them accountable to performance. It's giving them goals and objectives. It's giving them feedback on their performance. That's the management part of the job. It's the day-to-day guidance and supervision of your people.

The leadership part of your job is about establishing a vision, outlining a strategy, and inspiring, motivating, coaching, and developing people.

The terms managing and leading are often used interchangeably, but they are not the same thing. They're two different parts of your role. Early in your career, management is the majority of your job. The further you move up in your career, the more that starts to shift. You go from supervising to managing, to managing other managers, and to managing executives. The graph below illustrates the parameters of this shift. Managing and leading add up to 100%, and technical and business/strategic competence add up to 100%. It's not an exact science, as there are a number of factors that could impact this—size of your firm, your team(s), industry, health of the business, etc.:

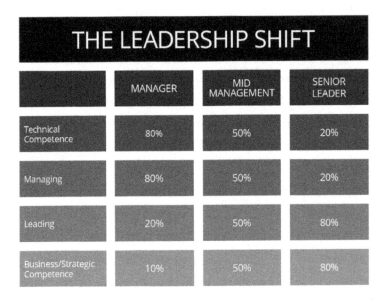

THE LEADERSHIP SHIFT			
	MANAGER	MID MANAGEMENT	SENIOR LEADER
Technical Competence	80%	50%	20%
Managing	80%	50%	20%
Leading	20%	50%	80%
Business/Strategic Competence	10%	50%	80%

Source: Chuck Mollor

The shifts we're going to talk about in the next chapters can be difficult for someone who's been successful. I'm not suggesting that you abandon everything that has gotten you to where you are today; I am challenging you to evolve.

Take your formula for success and tweak it. Make the necessary modifications and find a new and improved formula that will carry you to the next stage of success. Continue to be open to that change, modify, and adjust throughout your career.

You may be a manager, a mid-level executive, or a C-level executive. You may be managing people who were once your peers. You may be managing other leaders. All of these role shifts require updates to your formula. *A leader who can shift is an Agile Leader.*

Moving from You to Them

At this point in your career, you may have spent most of your effort maintaining visibility—trying to get noticed for your performance, your results, and your expertise. You're the person who's always taking on extra projects. You volunteer for visible initiatives and strategic task forces and go the extra mile.

You put yourself in positions that allow people to see what you're doing. You always raise your hand. You present to leadership or customers. You've been learning all you can, doing what you can to advance. But now you've come to a point in your career where that's no longer necessary.

I started having children in my mid-late thirties and I am now fortunate to have four wonderful children. But I remember when I first got married, that was a big shift for me because I went from being the center of my own universe to now sharing that center with somebody else. And that's a big change.

Going from being on my own to having a serious relationship was a major shift. When we had children, that was another shift. I went from being the center of my universe, to sharing that center, to suddenly realizing that my children became the center of my universe. My world flipped upside down.

If you have children, you can probably relate to that shift. Even if you don't, you can imagine the idea. You're no longer in the center of your universe. Your kids are. In a similar way, once you move into leadership, you are no longer the center of your universe.

Now that you have advanced in your career, you've got to make the same shift. Now, your people, your organization, and your company have to become the center of your universe. Shift from you being front-and-center to bringing your people forward. A good leader knows how to move into the background and give others the opportunity to develop and shine. *You have to make this shift from you to them.*

Managing Your Time

Another shift you have to make is time management. As you increase your leadership roles and responsibilities in your career, you need to spend more time being strategic and externally focused, as opposed to spending your time involved in the day-to-day. Spending time speaking with customers, experts in the field, other executives, and competitors, and identifying trends and industry disruptors is critical. **Too many leaders today are too internally focused.**

If you talk to most successful executives and leaders, they will tell you that time management is one of the most critical elements to their success.

I give an exercise to many of my clients, and it reveals exactly where they spend their time. Many leaders think they know how they spend their time but are surprised by the results of this exercise.

It's very simple. Just print out your calendar for the last two or three months. You may have a few atypical weeks in there, but it should give you a good general idea of what your work schedule looks like.

Now that you have your calendar in front of you, divide your time into buckets. How much of your time is focused externally? How much of your time is strategic? How much of your time is with other senior executives in the organization, or your peers, or your boss? And then how much of your time is the day-to-day or operational meetings? How much time do you block off for self-development and self-reflection?

Almost everybody comes back to me in disbelief after doing this exercise. They have this self-perception of being strategic. Of being external. Of creating time to think, reflect, plan, and be strategic. But the calendar doesn't lie, and it usually tells a different story. They realize they have a disconnect between how they think they spend their time, and what they actually do day-to-day.

It's a highly effective technique because it's so easy for executives to simply get dragged from meeting to meeting. It feels necessary to say yes to all the requests for time. We all need to learn how to say no or to delegate to someone else! Delegating is a gift. You get more time back, and someone else gains valuable experience. You can't be so accommodating and available all the time. Yes, it can be a struggle to be accessible versus spending time where you need to be. The answer, though, is not to add 10-20+ hours a week to be externally focused and strategic, and to add time to think, plan, and reflect. I have executive clients who have tried this and, to no surprise, were on the road to burnout. It's impossible to sustain. Remember, *time, and where you spend it, is one of your most precious gifts.*

Another critical shift, where applicable, is to hire a strong and effective administrative/executive assistant. This can make a huge difference between a good leader and a great leader. A good assistant will help you manage your calendar. Everyone wants you, everyone wants meetings, everyone wants to get in front of you, and everyone wants you involved in decisions.

This has to stop. You can't become bottlenecked. You can't go to meetings all day long. You'd be surprised how many leaders do that, and a solution is a good assistant. Your assistant should be your gatekeeper. When you're managing other people, you need an assistant who helps manage requests and the flow of communication; a good administrative assistant will reroute requests for meetings, visits, and appointments.

I can see the difference between a leader who operates like a well-oiled machine with time management when they have a great assistant, versus a talented leader who struggles with their calendar and time management. Often, they have a struggling assistant, if they have one at all.

Be sure to have an assistant who understands and can manage your time in an empathic, organized, and effective way. I have also seen far too many leaders, including CEOs, who feel they don't need an administrative/executive assistant at all—a big mistake and another reflection of not spending time where you need to. *Make the shift.*

It's tempting to think, "Oh, you know, I don't need all of that, I just manage my own calendar." It's more important to take a strategic approach and delegate, rather than to think you can or should manage everything yourself. This is all part of the leadership shift.

Your time is precious. This truth is starting to resonate with people. We are all running a hundred miles an hour, all connected through social media. We've got our emails on our devices and we can take our work anywhere.

Before the internet, we used to go on vacation and really get away. Now you go on vacation, but you can have your phone and your laptop and can be constantly connected. So you have to force yourself to protect your time and to know when to shut down and let it go.

Today, people can communicate on a much more intense and more frequent basis, whether it's through emails, texts, phone calls, or video. It's so easy to get sucked into the day to day. And let's face it, when you're in an earlier management role, you are more operationally focused. The further you move up the ladder in management, the more you have to shift and be more strategic, less operational. Many senior managers struggle with feeling they need to be in the know; they think they need to be involved in the day-to-day.

That's part of evolving your formula for success. When you start advancing, if you continue to be too hands-on with the day-to-day, you are risking failure. *Understand what success is at the level you are at!*

I work with a lot of executives that are getting promoted into senior, C-level positions. One of their biggest challenges is, "How do I shift on where I spend my time every day? How do I become more strategic and externally focused? How do I become more relationship-focused with my subordinates, peers, boss, or with the board?"

Letting go of the day-to-day is highly uncomfortable for most people. It feels easy and safe to be a micromanager, to think, "I have to be involved in every decision or everything will fall apart." But if you spend more of your time on the big picture, it gives others a chance to excel. A big part of this shift is letting go, not needing to be in the know about everything. You are accelerating and shifting ownership of decision making and responsibilities to your direct reports, and they need to do the same with their direct reports, and so on. If you are not making this shift, you are becoming a barrier for decision making and are conditioning your people to run to you for most, if not all, decisions. You want to have your people be able to think things through on their own, involve their peers, direct reports, and other stakeholders. Yes, they can bounce ideas off you and you make some decisions, but your people need to know the parameters on what to involve you in and what not to, recognizing that could change often.

The *leadership shift* is so critical. You need to shift how you develop and empower others, how you create time for self-reflection and development, how to be more externally focused, how you spend time being strategic and developing best practices, and how you take the time to build strong relationships and alliances across the organization and enterprise.

Chapter 11: The Art of Asking Questions

Most managers tell people what to do and you move up in your career by being the one who gets things done. You help build a business or operation, or produce a product, solution, service, or tool. You overcome obstacles and execute.

After being the person who does things, when you shift into management you begin telling people what you've done, how you did it, and how they should do it. You're probably spending at least 80% of your time talking. In order to become more effective as a *leader*, you need to shift your focus from telling to asking, to *facilitating dialogue*.

Most leaders should be able to shift to asking questions about 70-80% of the time and giving instructions about 20-30% of the time. That can be a hard shift for most leaders who are used to leading the charge over the hill.

The leader of today and tomorrow can't be a command-and-control leader. They need to empower people, teams, and organizations to be agile and innovative. They need to create a culture with a *growth mindset*. Employees at growth mindset companies feel more committed to their work because they feel they have the potential to grow, thrive, and innovate within their organization. A growth mindset can be highly transformable in any organization and ensures agility in today's evolving business and technological environments. Satya Nadella, CEO of Microsoft, has embraced this philosophy to transition the tech giant from a *"know it all"* to a *"learn it all"* work environment.

Going from being the general issuing orders to being a leader facilitating dialogue between your people is a critical shift. I'm not saying you're going to completely stop leading the charge over the hill. There are moments when you have to do that, but on a day-to-day basis if you're always the point person and if you're always making decisions, you become a barrier to growth and decision making.

When you don't let go, everything goes through you by default, and you've *conditioned* the people around you to handle things that way. They are not making decisions because you have to be involved in everything. Part of shifting from managing to leading is learning to ask questions and to start empowering instead.

What if you start empowering people, but they don't know what you want? It starts with delegating effectively. Empowering means giving people some type of decision-making capability, allowing room to fall down, scrape their knees, and get back up again. Maybe they make mistakes, or fail, or make an error. They need to know that the learning process is okay. You've got to give people a chance. It's like birds leaving the nest. You've got to give people a chance to fall or fly.

Shift from being the teller and the doer. You may feel like you have all the answers and experience, like you're the expert with all your wisdom and savvy. You can easily tell a person what the answer is, but if you want to develop and empower them, you have to lead them down the path to find the answer for themselves. The only way to do that is to shift from giving orders to asking questions.

I've told leaders that if you get good at this, it will change your life! That sounds like a very dramatic statement, but it's true. It will take time, like anything else. But you'll stop being a bottleneck. You'll start engaging your employees, getting people to put in discretionary effort beyond the minimum job requirements.

For example, one client of mine was an amazing executive—inspirational, smart, and well-connected. She was turning around a struggling company and dove deep into the business so she could understand it and her people on multiple levels. She needed to shift to a higher, more strategic level, but she also needed to know everything that was going on, so she was involved in the day-to-day. At times, instead of delegating, she would just do the work herself. She was running at 100 miles an hour, making fast decisions, and telling people what to do and not do. It all caught up to her. Being in the trenches, she added 25+ hours to her week. She was so hands-on; it was beginning to burn her out. She was conditioning her people to run to her with all of their decisions, so she became a bottleneck since she couldn't keep up with all of the information and requests.

We worked hard together to develop the patience and awareness so her people would have greater ownership and stop running to her for all decision making. Eventually, she began to let go of the day-to-day and shifted her time to be more externally focused and to spend time developing stronger relationships across the enterprise and with her team. By asking questions, slowing down to observe, and guiding people down a path of ownership, she became a more powerful force and completely changed her effectiveness. As a result, her team and organization, as her direct reports, repeated this same leadership style with their teams, and so on.

If you want a highly empowered team and a highly engaged organization, teach other managers to shift from telling and doing to facilitating dialogue and asking questions. It's really one of the most powerful techniques and skills you can have as a leader.

Another major benefit of asking questions is getting to observe your person or team. You get to see how prepared they are and determine whether they have the necessary critical thinking skills. By holding off your opinion or decision in asking questions, you might learn something new or alter your view and decision. Facilitating dialogue through questions allows you to evaluate and guide your people down a certain path *so they can maintain ownership*! When you tell people what to do and how to do it, who owns it? You do.

When you ask and facilitate, you maintain ownership with the person or team you are speaking with—so critical! Let go of the need to control, to do it yourself, or to tell a person what to do because it's faster and more efficient.

Too many leaders are desperate to establish credibility with their organization and team, especially if they're new to the business. Many feel they have to tell people what they know and what they've done. They go around referencing their accomplishments to show that they know what they're doing. In an attempt to cover their insecurities about their new position, they overuse their ego with these displays of bravado.

The problem with declaring how great you are is that the people around you can often see exactly what you're doing. Instead of being impressed with the show, they see right through the curtain into your insecurities. The key here is to not declare who you are and what you've done, but to demonstrate it. *Demonstrate, don't declare.*

One of the most effective ways of demonstrating your expertise and knowledge is by asking the right questions. You show your competence, your strategic capability, your knowledge, and your vision not by telling, but by demonstrating it through asking questions.

Managing Key Stakeholders

When you shift from managing to leading, you go from managing just employees to managing employees and all your internal and external key stakeholders. These are your boss, your peers, your subordinates, and other key people in and outside of the organization, people that you have to work with closely. It's important to cultivate strong working relationships across the enterprise.

As you start moving up, you have to be much more effective in how you establish key relationships that are not always directly related with your day-to-day job.

As you advance your career, you've got to have a much more peripheral view of your organization, your company, your world, and the marketplace. That's another shift. It's not just managing key stakeholders effectively; it's shifting your focus from what you are responsible for to an enterprise focus.

Influence and Persuasion

Another important shift is how you influence and persuade. Many leaders try to influence and persuade during a meeting or a presentation, in front of an audience or their bosses, or attempt to introduce a new concept, or push back on someone's idea. Trying to influence and persuade at the moment is not the best tactic.

This approach is not effective because you're often catching people off guard, and worse, you have little or no idea of what their response will be. They may be expecting a typical progress report, and here you come with a great new idea. The risk level is very high for you as a leader because they haven't vetted you and you haven't vetted them. You're telling, not asking questions or facilitating dialogue. You haven't spent enough time understanding what works, and what people's viewpoints are behind the scenes.

I call influencing and persuading behind the scenes *the Capitol Hill effect*. Picture what happens in Congress. Someone gets up to present or debate a vote for a bill, and they're met with grandstanding and drama. It can come across like a soap opera with the accusations and tear-filled speeches.

The decisions have already been made. They've been meeting for weeks, if not longer, behind the scenes, negotiating and compromising the language of the bill. You support me here, I'll support you there.

The way *the Capitol Hill effect* applies to business is that you never show up to debate or vote and surprise people with what you're trying to influence them to do. You've got to get behind the scenes and understand what they're thinking, what they want to do, what they're interested in, and how they react to your thoughts.

That's a shift because most leaders have never had to worry about that kind of scenario before. As you gain a more influential role, you have to think about how to do this more effectively and more strategically. How can you have intentional conversations that create influence over time, and one-on-one?

Influence and persuasion become important skill sets as you move up in your career. When you're early in your career, you're probably not getting in front of the board; you can spring a new idea on your boss and get away with it.

As you move up in your career, expectations of your ability to influence, persuade and also *create alignment* are much higher. Anytime you're trying to influence a new idea, initiative, or direction, you have to go to your boss, or a group of people, and try to influence them.

To be successful, do your real work ahead of time, behind the scenes. Learn if they need time to process and kick the tires, or if they are comfortable with being direct. Develop relationships, know how people are likely to react, and plan for that. Influence and persuade people as individuals rather than as a group. Have conversations well in advance. Test theories, plant seeds, and identify likely initial reactions.

That puts you in a much better position to present your ideas, or to make your argument, etc. I'm not saying that you won't get pushback, or that people won't change their position, or that people won't challenge or ask questions, but at least now you'll be prepared.

Otherwise, you're going in blind and putting yourself at serious risk. Increase your ability to understand people's positions, reactions, and views, and vet them behind the scenes instead of putting all your cards on the table in one all important moment.

How to Influence and Persuade When You Don't Have Authority

The other critical area is influencing others when you have no direct authority or control over them. This is typically found in matrixed organizations, virtual teams, and outsourcing, but is rapidly spreading to most organizations. Either way, as a leader, you must be effective at this.

Your *attitude*, or how you treat other people, is one of the most important factors of influence regardless of your title. Be *honest and straightforward*. A slip in your integrity will cost you trust for a long time. *Don't waste people's time* - make sure you are prepared and organized.

Demonstrate respect; your tone of voice, your choice of words, and acknowledgment of challenging situations can be your most powerful influence.

Get to know people and form strong connections and *relationships*. Strong, healthy relationships are the foundation of trust and play a significant part in how you influence and are influenced. People who trust you will be much more willing to follow you. A *sense of camaraderie* goes a long way toward encouraging people to solve problems together and to win together.

Share your *vision, inspire,* and *motivate* people to want to be part of that vision.

Use your *expertise* to demonstrate credibility in how you influence others. Having a *track record* of results, achievement, success, and collaboration is a strong influencer. Recognize others' expertise and track record—people appreciate being *acknowledged*.

Information is most powerful when *shared*. Influence others by sharing the information you know regularly, clearly, and concisely. Gather it and share what you know. Sharing information by being transparent establishes trust and openness.

Have resources that you can leverage and share. Creative use of resources can be the difference between success and failure.

Do your homework and present your case and position. Articulate what you want to do and how things will improve or be better.

Establish *partnerships and alliances*. This could be a joint/ combined effort to develop new products or services.

Cooperation Builders

Given the challenges and complexities of managing through influence, what can leaders do to encourage and sustain cooperation?

Improve Communication and Transparency

When we communicate our intent to cooperate, we can increase the likelihood the other person will respond in kind. This, of course, assumes that our communication is clear, and our intentions are understood. Unfortunately, this is not always the case. Although people often act with good intent and do what they think is right, they are often unable to coordinate their actions because of a breakdown in communication.

The most common mistake is assuming the other person understands what we wanted or intended. It's helpful to develop the habit of being explicit about *why* you are doing something or making a request. Another mistake is not taking the time to do a "comprehension check" by asking questions to confirm the other person's perception of actions and next steps.

Agree on When Cooperation Is Needed and What It Looks Like

Lack of clarity about roles and responsibilities is another cooperation-crusher. It results in conflicts among team members or groups. It also allows key responsibilities to fall through the cracks because each party believes that someone else is responsible for them. In these situations, our level of cooperation is generally higher when everyone involved agrees on when it is needed and what it looks like. When we know what to expect from other people, we are more willing to trust them and take the risk of cooperation.

Although the process of discussing roles and reaching agreement takes time, it is well worth the investment. On their own, some teams may eventually come to an understanding about when and how to work together. Agreeing to roles at the early stage of a team's formation, or whenever you notice a lack of cooperation, helps accelerate the process and preserve trust.

Align Interests and Establish Common Ground

When the objectives of a person or group are at odds with those of another, cooperation and collaboration suffer. Picture the potential conflicts and inefficiencies that would result if one group in your department was working toward reducing costs, while another group was focused on bringing state-of-the-art products and services to market. These objectives can coexist, but most likely won't happen on their own. To facilitate alignment between the two groups, leaders must develop compatible and mutually supportive objectives in a thoughtful and explicit manner.

Disagreements Happen - How to Sustain Cooperation

Although cooperation builders provide a foundation to encourage teamwork, they won't eliminate disagreements about what to do and how to do it, and won't change the fact that people have different priorities, make mistakes, and sometimes fail to meet others' expectations. In order to sustain cooperation and collaboration, leaders must use influence to gain the support of others for their ideas, and effective conflict management skills to constructively resolve differences across organizational boundaries.

Influence with Impact

A leader's success often depends on their ability to gain the support and cooperation of people who have competing priorities and/or conflicting goals. The effective use of influence is the most powerful tool a leader has to create alignment and build commitment in these situations.

The ability to influence is not solely based on organizational hierarchy. There are four core tactics that are most closely associated with gaining commitment from others:

1. Rational Persuasion involves the use of explanations, logical arguments, and factual evidence to explain why a request or proposal will benefit the organization or help to achieve a vital task objective. The key to using rational persuasion is the ability to convert features into benefits *as seen by the person you are influencing.*

2. Inspirational Appeals involves an emotional or value-based appeal, in contrast to the logical arguments used in rational persuasion. While rational persuasion appeals to the "head,"

inspirational appeals focus on "the heart." A common misconception is that inspirational appeals require a leader to be "rah-rah" and highly charismatic. This is not the case. If a leader is effective at using rational persuasion, they can be just as effective at using inspirational appeals. The difference is that with inspirational appeals, benefits are positioned in a more value-oriented manner.

3. Consultation involves asking a person to suggest improvements or help plan a proposed activity or change for which their support is desired. With this tactic, the other person is invited to participate in planning how to carry out a request or implement a proposed change.

4. Collaboration involves offering to provide relevant resources or assistance if the other person will carry out a request or approve a proposed change. Like consultation, collaboration is participative, but the focus of collaboration is on reducing difficulty or costs of carrying out a request. This tactic is most effective with peers.

Manage Differences and Reach Agreement

The word "conflict" often conjures up images of confrontation and anger, but this is often not the case. Disagreements occur in even the most positive and productive work relationships—at least, they should. Conflict itself is neither inherently good nor bad—what is perceived as positive or negative is how the differences are managed and the outcome that results.

What does it take to manage conflict effectively? For one, conflict needs to be acknowledged. When conflict is brought to the surface, problems can be addressed, and people can take action to resolve issues. Many people avoid or minimize conflicts in an attempt to maintain harmonious relationships; this is a mistake because the problem may never be resolved. Many a solid long-term relationship is born from the difficult but constructive resolution of a conflict.

Another key to managing conflict is *clarifying the source* of the conflict. Differences of opinion concerning one or more of the following four issues will cause conflict to occur: facts, methods, goals, and values. Differences of *fact* are the most straightforward conflicts to resolve. Facts are concrete. They can be checked, compared, and tested, and this provides a basis for discussion and the exchange of information. Conflicts over facts can be resolved through dialogue more often than conflicts involving the other basic issues.

People may have similar goals and agree on the facts but may be unable to agree on ways to achieve their goals. However, shared goals mean that a logical, rational way of choosing among alternative approaches is possible—it's just a matter of convincing everyone that a particular method will achieve the goals at hand.

When the issue is related to *goals*, people have different objectives and may support different courses of action. Information sharing is the key to resolving conflicts over either methods or goals. It helps each person understand what is important to the other person.

Occasionally, when differing goals exist, a third person may be needed to determine which goal (or combination of goals) is most appropriate.

Conflicts arising from different values are most difficult to resolve. In fact, they are often not able to be resolved. People's beliefs tend to become inflexible over time and are often based on emotion rather than reason. Finding common ground and separating those that are not solvable from those that are, frequently moves such conflicts toward productive action.

Your mindset should be that people have the right to think or feel differently than you do and that you will benefit from developing solutions that will be acceptable and beneficial to everyone.

Conclusion

Organizations are complex structures with many interdependencies. We rely on others to help get things done and meet our objectives, and that means cooperation and collaboration are often the keys to our success. The challenge leaders face in the workplace is to ensure the conditions that create and sustain cooperation and collaboration are in place. This is even more challenging in a matrix structure.

Cooperation and collaboration are facilitated by clear communication, shared goals, and clearly defined roles. These conditions help encourage and motivate people to focus on the group's best interests without feeling that they are minimizing or trading off their interests in the process.

Once in place, however, cooperation is a delicate state. People will still have disagreements and different points of view about how and when things should happen. Leaders' ability to effectively and constructively influence others and gain their support is critical to maintaining cooperation.

Leaders who focus on these key areas will have much greater success in creating a culture of cooperation and achieving their business objectives in today's matrix organizations.

Chapter 12: Continual Self-Evaluation

Self-Reflection

As you are reframing your formula for success, you have considered and possibly implemented some important shifts in your thoughts and actions. You've started asking more questions, facilitating dialogue, moving your focus from you to them, looking for areas to influence, and making time for more strategic thinking and less day-to-day operational management.

Begin or ensure you are *consistently* taking time each week for *self-reflection*. Develop yourself as a leader. Find your voice. Help others find their voice!

> *"We do not learn from experience...we learn from reflecting on experience." – John Dewey*

This is important, because as a leader, you have to be in continual evaluation mode. You are evaluating others, goals, strategies, structure, and the business, but you are also evaluating yourself. Knowing the basic tenets of good leadership is only useful if you take a step back, look at your own life and work, see ways to improve, and then make those improvements.

You can go to conferences, watch webinars, and listen to podcasts on leadership all you want, but if you never evaluate your own leadership and do what is necessary to get better, you won't.

Essentially, if you can't lead yourself into a better, more effective future, how will you lead others? How will you lead your organization, your company?

Any time you do any kind of leadership development, whether it's coaching, a conference, program, training, or assessment, schedule some time immediately upon your return to think through what you've learned. Come up with a list of two or three things that you're working on as a leader and have a plan of action on what you will work on—what will change or be different, what improvement or success will look like.

We've already talked about how self-improvement is like going to the gym: you might know you need to get into better shape, and you might even have a membership, but if you don't go to the gym and do the workouts, you're not going to strengthen your muscles or improve your cardiovascular health.

Only going once and working out for five hours isn't effective either. You're going to be burnt out and sore—you might not get out of bed for a week, you probably won't go back, and therefore you won't see results.

It's the people who go consistently and work out over a period of time who start seeing measurable improvement, not only in how they look and feel, but in their actual strength and physical health.

Becoming effective as a leader is no different; just because you know what you need to do doesn't mean you do it. Maybe you went through a coaching program and acquired all this knowledge. Now you have to take that knowledge and actually develop yourself. Change your habits. Maybe add some new ones.

Just like going to the gym, if you're not working consistently on what you need to improve, the improvement won't happen. You can spend all the money you want on coaching or courses, but it's a waste if you do nothing with it. *Just because you know, it doesn't mean you do!* Modifying behaviors and developing behaviors, knowledge, skills, and techniques is not a light switch moment.

Once you have been on your path of improved awareness of yourself and others, and developed action items to improve yourself as a leader, dust off prior documentation of triggers to see how you are progressing; be intentional in continually reviewing current behaviors versus desired behaviors. Continue teaming up with trusted colleagues to ensure there's no slipping back into prior habits.

Behavior-Changing Exercise

When I was only a few years out of college, I was in a manager training program at a consulting firm. Five of us went to one of the owners of the firm in New York City. This terrific gentleman put us in a very intensive one-week video training program to improve our effectiveness in developing our presence, how we interacted with others, and business relationships. As we can all attest, videotape training is so much fun, since we just love watching ourselves on video...

For at least four full days we became acutely aware of all our bad habits (the "you know's," the "ah's," bad body language, etc.) and learned new approaches and techniques. We practiced them on video, evaluating each other, time after time for nine hours a day. It's a painful, tedious type of training. It's also very powerful because you see yourself and all your bad habits.

We were working to improve our presentation skills, body language, posture, eye contact, tone of voice, all those things. We were all in our twenties, the up-and-coming hotshots of the business world.

We knew we were making major progress; it was all there on video. We had been learning and practicing for days, feeling very confident, even a bit cocky. On the evening before the last day, we were having a very nice graduation dinner when our host gave us one more assignment.

We each had one or two particularly bad habits we had been working on all week, whether it was a gesture or nonsense word.

He instructed us to pair up the next morning when we went back to work, and that if our partner displayed any of their bad habits, we would simply tap them on the shoulder. He told us to practice for an hour or so, and then meet back at lunch to let him know how it went.

We all thought it would be a piece of cake. Here we'd been in this intense training, practicing all this on video, doing the same things over and over for days. We had this down. We knew what to do. We all thought maybe he was starting to lose his touch.

We came back the next morning and paired up. I think I was two minutes into the day when I felt the first tap on my shoulder. Five minutes later, it happened again. This continued in the first 20 minutes or so. I started paying more attention and tried to recalibrate. I still got tapped a few more times, maybe eight times total, and I was devastated. I thought I was done for. I tapped my partner ten times.

We all got together a few minutes before lunch with the firm owner and started comparing, quickly coming to the realization that we had all bombed! Some of us had six shoulder taps, some had fourteen. We thought, "wow, what a bunch of inept young hot-shots! Couldn't pass a simple test after a week of intensive training." We were a bit embarrassed.

We started to panic, thinking we were going to get kicked out of this company. Still stuck in the same habits after working on them for four straight days? We knew we were in trouble. We'd started the day feeling great, but now we just felt stupid. We were dreading lunch.

When the time came to meet with the owner, we were all feeling very sheepish and didn't want to talk. He came in, smiled, and asked, "How did it go?" We looked at each other and finally one brave soul admitted it hadn't gone well. Then we all spilled the beans and waited for him to tell us what failures we were.

Instead, he smiled and said that was exactly what he'd expected. He told us he wanted us to see that changing habits or tendencies is incredibly hard, even when you know what you need to change and work on it. And that lesson has stuck with me, especially when I began coaching leaders. I use this story with clients to understand how hard it really is to modify and improve behavior and derailers, especially when they are deeply rooted.

Much of leadership development is about behavioral modification, including where you spend your time and how you make all these shifts we're talking about. But that story always stuck with me because it really is a practical example of how just because you know what to do, you might not always do it. It takes a long time. It takes a lot of hard work. It takes practice. It takes feedback!

You need to deliberately take time for self-reflection and self-development. Put it on your calendar. Make an appointment with yourself and protect that time. Don't fall to the temptation of thinking you'll get to it when you have time, because you won't. Again, it's like the gym—you have to be intentional about it.

Provide and ask for real-time feedback to help with accountability and enable the "tap on the shoulder." Ask a few peers, subordinates, or colleagues with whom you work closely. It's okay if you are not very friendly as long as there is mutual respect and they will be straight with you.

That seems simple and maybe a little off-putting, but it's truly a powerful tool for those who are willing to use it. It causes a shift because as a leader, you're used to being in charge and having all of the answers, decisions, and feedback. You might find it difficult to ask others for feedback because you're the one who's supposed to know everything.

Being open to feedback shows vulnerability and empathy, and that's very important. If you're not open to feedback, why would you expect your people to be? We all get defensive. We all have insecurities. We'd all rather prove how much we know than humbly ask questions. When you're asking for input and feedback, you're showing that you're learning, and that you can be open to change.

The Halo Effect

It's human nature. You are up for a raise, bonus, or promotion and you are on your best behavior until you receive it. When you are provided feedback or are asked to participate in a management or leadership development program, including executive coaching, the same thing can happen. I refer to this as the *halo effect*; putting on your best face and being at your behavioral best due to the spotlight being put on you. And once the development program has ended or the feedback received is in the past, you go back to your "regular" self. To avoid the halo effect, truly internalize the feedback and development. Do something about it and create a plan for how you will work on your development needs each week, so it is not an "event." The goal is to turn it into sustainable focus and improvement.

Avoidance

It's human nature to avoid dealing with feedback you have received or the suggestion of going through a development program (executive coaching, executive program, or leadership development course). Don't put off and delay what you need in order to get to the next level of your leadership development. The patterns of gaps, needs, and development opportunities won't go away. We know the excuses: I'm too busy, I will get to it eventually, etc. "Eventually" never happens. Create the time and begin to make changes now.

Decompress

We move 100 miles an hour, our schedules are jammed, and there are people, organizations, structures, deliverables, and client issues. You feel like you are slowly starting to slide down a very slippery slope and the light at the end of the tunnel starts to become smaller. You are driving to work and then home each day, and thanks to modern technology, you are on the phone with staff, clients, vendors, etc. The problem? When do you *decompress*? We all need to do it but it's tough to find the time.

Our ability to effectively manage pressure and stress is critical. Some of that is impacted by how well we take care of ourselves: getting enough sleep, eating healthy, spending time with family and friends, exercise, time for hobbies and passions, taking time off and vacations, etc. Some of it is about creating time on our calendar for thinking, reflecting, and planning. There isn't a successful leader who has not learned how to do this. It's critical. It's the *shift* of where you spend your time and how effectively you empower and delegate to your people.

How do you show up in front of people? If you are running from meeting to phone call to meeting all day long, especially when those meetings can be brutal calls or conversations with a client, vendor, boss, or staff, when do you collect yourself? Have a moment to decompress? Take a deep breath. Gather yourself and your composure.

One mistake I used to make quite often was to finish calls as I walked into my house. The problem with that was I have a wife, children, and dogs who all wanted to engage and connect with me when I got home. All I wanted to do was find a chair and a quiet room to decompress. I found out that wasn't working, so I learned to stop most of my calls, if I could, a few minutes before I walked into my house, so I could decompress and gather my composure. If

I was on a call as I was entering my garage, I would wait a minute before entering my home. Now, if you are like me and you're not an extrovert (I'm not an introvert either), it's even more important to decompress, as you have to stretch your extroversion to connect with people.

Chapter 13: Be Whole

What is it to *be whole*? How do we know what wholeness means, and what does it have to do with leadership?

The best leaders know that success is about more than work. Think about your life in four areas: your personal self, your family, your work, and your community. There is a lot of talk these days about work/life balance. The dilemma is it's a very subjective idea.

What does "balance" really mean? It's important to understand this, because it ties into personal happiness and success — which are closely related to wholeness. To be effective as a leader, you've got to be whole.

So, let's discuss this idea of balance. When we think of work/life balance, it's easy to think balance means 50/50. Or possibly, if we're thinking in terms of those quadrants I previously laid out, it's a 25/25/25/25 split.

However, reality doesn't look that way. Sometimes we over-rotate to one quadrant. Some leaders are so rotated to their work that they are not healthy, they're not spending enough quality time with their family, they're not active at all in their community, and worst, they're not taking care of themselves emotionally, spiritually, physically, or mentally. You know the old cliché: If you don't take care of yourself, you can't take care of the world around you.

But being able to take care of your world is a foundation of leadership. So, no, you cannot sacrifice yourself for the good of others. That is a one-way route to failure, unhappiness, and possibly illness.

Instead, strive for a more realistic definition of balance. That means making sure you're spending quality time and interaction in each quadrant. It doesn't necessarily mean equal time or effort in each, as long as the needs being met can balance out. Make sure that you're spending time with your family, with your community, and personal "you" time, along with adequate time and energy at work.

Being whole is important, and balance is how you achieve it. This doesn't mean that you're going to be wholly investing in every arena equally, every day and every week. Because of the way life is, you're going to have some seasons when you are out of balance. You may be in a particular phase where you may have to prioritize one quadrant over the rest for a time. The key is to come out of this phase and restore "balance" and wholeness with the other quadrants.

I think of this process of stepping back and evaluating your four quadrants like a recalibration. There will be times in your leadership when you'll need to recalibrate a few things. So, how do you recalibrate? How do you make that shift of where you spend your time?

Every once in a while, press pause, take a step back, and evaluate each of the areas of your life. You may find, as you reflect, that it's time to recalibrate your schedule, your attention, and even your investments of time and resources, so you can move out of imbalance and work toward being whole.

For example, one often-overlooked quadrant is your personal self. It can be hard to focus on yourself because it feels selfish, petty, or even wasteful; you feel that people are counting on you! Opt out of this mindset because it's not what will make you whole. Instead, ask yourself if you are spending enough time on yourself and what makes you happy. Are you spending time on any hobbies or interests? Or on your spirituality, your emotions, and your relationships? Are the relationships you're in bringing out the best in you? If not, you may need to take a step back.

Remember: It's normal to resist this emphasis on self and happiness. Rewrite that script and decide that it's okay to focus on yourself sometimes. It's not only okay, I'd argue that it's necessary.

Here's why: When you are whole and healthy, taking care of yourself, you can be more present in the other quadrants, as well. What the other three have in common… is you.

We all know the mantra of living a life of no regrets and not looking back at your life when you are near the end, and saying, "I wish I had done this or had done that."

What Really Matters?

Being whole means you take time to focus on yourself, which allows you to manage the most important aspects of your life:

Health. If you don't have your health, energy, strength, and passion, how will you impact the world around you? Are you getting enough rest and sleep? Do you find time to decompress or take vacations? Are you eating healthy?

Emotions. Are you in a good place emotionally? Are you constantly angry or frustrated? Are you consistently relaxed, at ease, in control of your emotions?

Relationships. Do you have strong, open, trusting, loyal, and intimate relationships? Are you spending time with the right people who share similar values, priorities, and interests? Are the people around you bringing out the best in you?

Time. Are you spending time where you should? With your family and friends? On your interests, passions?

Spirituality. It's not about who or what you believe in, it's about feeding your soul and spirit. Take time to be thankful and appreciative of the world around you and the beauty around us. Mind-fulness gets a lot of buzz these days, for good reasons. Are you at peace with yourself, your family, your friends, and your colleagues?

Your health and ability to be physically and mentally healthy and sharp, are very important factors. And not only for your life and your personal life, but also in leadership.

Some other questions you can ask yourself to assess your self-health are:

- How much stress do I have, and how am I managing it?
- How am I managing my physical, emotional, mental, and spiritual health?
- How am I figuring out what makes me happy?
- Do I like myself? People can really struggle with them-selves, going back to the two-sided coin.
- Am I accepting myself for who I am?
- Am I doing something every day that I enjoy?
- Do I have things to look forward to?

I want to address a couple of key things. The first is self-ac-ceptance because it's something we don't talk about enough. I've found that it's a critical element of agile leadership.

As a leader, you've got to show up and be present, fully accept-ing of yourself and others. That doesn't mean you are not going to push, stretch, and challenge others to reach their full potential (just as you are doing with yourself). Demonstrate to others that it's okay to be you, no matter who you are, what your background is, or what you look like. We all tend to be self-critical, which is why self-acceptance in leadership is so important. This is an example you need to set and if you're able to, it will benefit your entire organi-zation. *Walk the talk.*

Another thing to touch on is stress management. Life is a journey of finding and understanding what health is, and how it looks and feels. The demands placed on you will shift as time passes, but one thing that's near-constant is stress. This is especially true of leaders today.

Leaders have a lot of responsibilities and pressures, which can create a lot of stress. Stress management is a huge health factor, and it impacts who shows up as a leader. This makes your ability to manage stress all the more critical. How do you press the proverbial pause button? How do you manage your triggers? Those are all stress-related as well.

I find I have things I need to do to be able to help manage my stress and to decompress. For me, exercise is a huge factor. I also have to get enough sleep. If I don't get enough sleep and if I don't exercise, I have a hard time managing myself, my triggers, and my stress. It's important to figure out what things work for you.

Ultimately, this care-of-self paradigm is about how you live your life. Are you living the life you want to be living? If you aren't, step back and ask yourself why not. And further, ask yourself what you're going to do to make changes. These changes can be difficult and may take time. Focus on *incremental change*—you can't get there all at once. You will then move in the right direction.

I'm not saying you can be happy with everything all the time, or even that you should be. But there's a sense of happiness that comes with being mindful of accepting yourself. Once you can accept yourself, you can figure out what makes you happy. And by accepting yourself and others, by managing your triggers, by spending time being whole in all four of your quadrants, you will be well on your way to finding happiness.

What Are the Keys to Happiness?

Here's a very simple exercise for being whole and finding happiness: Write down your dreams, your goals, and your aspirations. What are your dreams? What are the things that are going to make you happy, not just for today, but for the future? What is most important to you? What are you aspiring to be? What is your purpose? What does that question even mean to you? Map it out so you can see it visually. What story is it telling you? It may take years or a lifetime to understand what happiness is for you, and how important it is to you.

What is your measure of success? Happiness, satisfaction, or legacy? Helping others be happy? It's difficult to make others "happy" if you're not happy yourself.

Here are five things you can do that can immediately increase the amount of happiness or satisfaction in your life.

Start each day with a positive expectation. Don't set yourself up for a *self-fulfilling prophecy*. Yes, if you feel something positive is going to happen, that's a good thing. That mindset can help something positive to happen! But on the other side of that coin, if you believe something bad is going to happen, you can set yourself up to help ensure a bad thing will happen. Which do you choose? When you wake up tomorrow, start your first thought with: "Something good is going to happen today." If you believe it, there is a good chance it will happen.

The opposite is also true. Allow yourself to be receptive to positive experiences. When you are disappointed or when something negative does happen (because that's life, it's not perfect and things go wrong), accept it and move on; learn from it.

Take time to think, plan, and prioritize. Accepting that you are too busy and that you will eventually get to what you want or need to do is really just an excuse. Telling yourself or others that you don't have time to do the things you really want or need to do—to improve yourself, take that vacation, see that friend, or do that project you've wanted to do—will one day cause you to look back with regret on the life you could have had.

You will not eventually get to it. Be honest with yourself. The only thing that can impact this is taking ownership of your life, routine, and schedule, and changing it! Create time for yourself. Block it out on your calendar! Pick one thing. If you get it done today, it will move you closer to your highest goal and purpose in life.

Steve Jobs, the founder of Apple, with all of his success, wealth, and legacy, is quoted near his death saying that the biggest regret of his life was not spending enough time with his family and friends.

Remember, quality of life and work/life balance means having time (*quality* time) with your family and friends, your work, your community, and yourself.

Give to everyone you meet. Give a smile, a word of thanks or encouragement, a gesture of politeness, or a friendly nod. Be kind—ask someone how they're doing or if there is anything you can do to help. Be present—focus on the person you are interacting with as if that interaction is the most important experience you will have that day. Don't be distracted by your tablet, phone, computer, etc.

Learn from others, regardless of who they are—young or old, an inexperienced or seasoned worker. Regardless of the level of success you might have achieved, be humble, grateful, and thankful. Demonstrate respect.

Let go. Forgive. The biggest enemies of happiness are worry, paranoia, hate, jealousy, judgment, guilt, and arrogance. Focus on what you can do moving forward. Learn from the past. Adjust. Focus on what you can control. You will make mistakes and fail. That's how you grow and learn. Forgive yourself. Others close to us will fail, make mistakes, even disappoint us. Forgive others. Rid yourself of what's holding you down. Let go. Free yourself of burden. It's hard to demonstrate love, acceptance, and respect for others if you don't do the same for yourself.

End each day with gratitude. Before you go to bed, write down one wonderful thing that happened that day. It might be making a child laugh, reaching out to a loved one, or winning that big deal. Whatever it is, be grateful for that moment and what it meant to you. What did it mean to others? How will it impact you tomorrow?

Do what makes you happy. To you, happiness may just be a 15-minute walk with someone that you really care about, down a beach, on a sidewalk, or in a park. What is true happiness? It isn't always about the big things. Don't get to the end of your life and regret the life you didn't live. Live that life. It won't be perfect. You will make mistakes, but can you live with yourself? Can you live with your imperfections? Recalling the two-sided coin, remember the need for self-acceptance and the acceptance of others.

As a leader, you have to manage yourself—your health and happiness, your work, your relationships, and your community involvement. But as a leader, it's part of your responsibility. How are you going to help others if you can't help yourself?

Be a leader in life—with yourself, your family, your friends, and your community.

Chapter 14: Can You Ride the Wave?

Let me give you a visual. Imagine a surfer on a surfboard out in the ocean. As we know, waves are completely unpredictable and unstable. In order to surf successfully, you have to be able to ride any wave that comes. You need balance, strength, stability, and focus. You have to be able to adapt to the waves and the weather. You need to be quick, flexible, and steady. You need to be agile.

When I work with leaders, I use this visual. There is so much in business and in life that is as unpredictable and chaotic as ocean waves. The best leaders know this and adapt accordingly. Do you have the ability to maintain stability in the midst of chaos? Can you *ride the wave?*

Please Fail

In riding the wave, the fear of failure can be a motivator, but can also paralyze you if you are not controlling your emotions. We often act as though failure is the worst possible thing that could happen to us, our people, or in our organizations—but is it?

If you look back at your life, have you learned more from your successes or your failures? What experiences shape us the most? Often, it is our failures and mistakes. It's when something didn't go well, or at least didn't go the way we planned.

Sometimes, we forget that. Success and innovation are often the result of a series of lessons learned through our experiments and failures. The good news is a failure is a moment in time—it's temporary. Bill Gates once put it this way: "Success is a lousy teacher. It seduces smart people into thinking they can't lose."

You can't grow unless you fail. It goes back as far as learning to walk, and you repeat some version of the same learning process throughout life. You fall, pick yourself up, and try again. It's the same for all of us. You, your clients, and the people who work with you and for you.

Think about Walt Disney. In his early twenties, Disney was fired from a Missouri newspaper for "not being creative enough." Then in 1921, he founded his first animation studio, Laugh-O-Gram Studio in Missouri. It went bankrupt within two years. It was only after this failure that Disney decided to move west to pursue his dreams in Hollywood. The rest, as they say, is history.

You have to create an environment where people are not afraid to fail or to take risks. It's ok if not everything is a "home run." This is really the critical piece because most leaders have gotten to where they are because they've overcome their failures. They have overcome their mistakes, so much so that they sometimes forget that they made them and that their response to those mistakes is probably what got them into leadership in the first place.

Sometimes leaders face too much pressure for success, wins, and achievement. We have to meet goals and have a long list of accomplishments. We forget what got us where we are—and what will continue to get us to where we need to be—is learning from our failures and difficult experiences. We have to be accommodating and open, receptive to that same process for the world around us and the people who work for us. Give people permission, even encouragement, to make mistakes and learn from them. Allow them to experiment. Make mistakes and fail, adjust, and try again. We have to be patient as failing, adjusting, and learning to be successful is a process, not an overnight sensation.

This is one of a leader's most interesting conflicts and tensions: the pressure of execution, success, growth, and wins. But in order to get there, they have to have a capacity to allow for errors and mistakes. They have to create a culture where people are not afraid. Because what happens when people are afraid to fail? They stop trying. Are they going to go the extra mile? Or take any risks? Of course not. In a culture where failure is part of the journey to success, people can admit their mistakes and not be sanctioned at work for them.

I work with many CEOs, and right now every CEO is trying to figure out how to be more innovative. The world is changing constantly. The customer is changing constantly. Their attitudes, their needs, and their appetites are always changing. Everything moves faster. There is an expectation—and therefore a demand—for immediate success.

Every company is dealing with that pressure in some way. As a result, everyone wants to be innovative, faster, and more agile; to not only pivot but pivot faster. Customers demand it, so executives demand it.

If you think about it, innovation is built on failure. And yet we often demand the opposite. We expect perfection. If you're naturally skeptical and/or naturally risk-averse, how do you modify that behavior?

If you provide a negative or punitive response to failures and mistakes, are your people going to be innovative or take risks?

Yes, as a CEO you want to be innovative, but here's the dynamic: if you want innovation, you must create innovative teams. If you want to have creative products and ideas, but the moment there are failures, mistakes, and errors, you balk and say, "no, we can't have that," people get reprimanded, and even lose jobs.

What happened in those situations? The leaders took innovation out of the organizational culture, but they didn't create a safe work environment, as we discussed in chapter 3.

We forget how we became innovative. We were able to advance our careers because we were not only risk-takers, we thought out of the box. We were resilient and overcame our fears, obstacles, challenges, and mistakes, and we challenged the status quo. But sometimes the pressure of leadership changes us. Early in our careers, we feel we have nothing to lose. As we advance in life and in work, the stakes get higher. When you get into leadership, sometimes you tend to forget that.

You have to realize that you may have people who are risk-averse on your team. Not everyone is comfortable with risk, uncertainty, and failure. Using tools like PI, you can determine which of your people are risk-takers or risk averse. That will allow you to understand how you should approach them differently about taking risks, addressing compliance, and making errors and mistakes. Make sure you know where you stand with this as well. We can all modify ourselves situationally, but it becomes increasingly difficult if you are trying to be someone you are not eight hours a day, five days a week.

Don't forget to allow failure. Fail fast, adjust, fail again, and repeat. Ask for it. Tell your people, "Please fail." Then, see how growth happens.

Have You Arrived?

When riding that wave, thinking about the future and losing focus of what's happening at the moment can have consequences. When you become overconfident, you leave yourself susceptible to having the wave knock you off your board.

For some, having the next career goal in mind is very important —and that's a good thing. If you're not advancing, you might feel that you're stagnant or retreating. There is a clear benefit of tackling challenging goals that stretch you and your team and provide you with the motivation for continued organizational and personal development.

Do you know what it means to *have arrived*? It can actually mean many things. Essentially, for our purposes, it means you've arrived at the pinnacle of your career. You've become an expert. You've got the title, prestige, and maybe the money and power that comes with it.

You want to avoid *"I've arrived."* This is a state of mind in which you feel you have reached the height of your knowledge and expertise; that you have reached the top of the mountain; that you are now a success story. It's a very dangerous place to be, as you are telling those around you that there is nothing else for you to learn, that you are above feedback and input because you have "arrived."

It can also mean you're no longer receptive to input or feedback. No one can teach you anything because you have all the answers. You also don't have to adapt, change, or modify. This is an extreme description of the arrival mindset. It doesn't always happen this way, but it can happen to anyone at varying degrees.

Feeling that you've "arrived" is something every leader has to guard against. It's tempting to sit back and bask in your success. Often, leaders who embrace this mentality become arrogant or conceited. But success is not a permanent state, and overconfidence can quickly lead to complacency and failure, especially in today's rapidly changing market.

Continue to realize that you do not have all the answers, ideas, and decision-making power. You will always be on a path of learning, improving, and becoming more self-aware and aware of the world around you. You will continue your lifelong path and journey of leadership effectiveness.

Resist the temptation to think you've arrived. Always be ready to learn from anyone. Combine confidence with humility and receptiveness, and you are much more likely to continue your track record of success.

Don't Take the Bait

When riding that wave, don't take the bait. There will always be people around you who try to take advantage of you in some way. It's unfortunately part of human nature. We want to believe that all people are ultimately good, but there are some who have ulterior motives.

How do you react to someone who clearly has an agenda? It might be political. It might be a form of greed or competitiveness. It might be that someone is threatened by you; there is something you have that they want, whether it's support, money, your best employees, or land-grabbing—and they will do what they can to get it. They will set you up or try to antagonize you. *Don't take the bait.* Don't allow yourself to retaliate, get *triggered*, defensive, or caught up in someone else's agenda.

An example I use with many executives is an analogy about golf. Even though I'm a big fan of the game and an avid golfer, you don't need to be a golfer to understand this. One of the keys to hitting a golf ball well is staying relaxed; keeping your arms, forearms, and hands relaxed; keeping your mind clear and present. You will hit the golf ball farther when you are relaxed and take a smooth swing and are centered and balanced. If you try to hit the golf ball as hard as possible, grip the club as tight as possible, and are off balance, the ball will not go very far or straight. Life and leadership are very similar. We excel when we are under control, measured, centered, balanced, and relaxed; when our minds are clear and present. But when we try to force things, press too hard, and are distracted, we lose our balance and our impact is not very effective or successful.

Can You Rise?

Riding the wave means *rising* above the minutia, the politics, the distractions, and the temptations that come your way as a leader. These can crash over you as quickly and unexpectedly as the crest of an ocean wave. Your ability to ride the wave depends on not giving in and letting any of these things topple you. Instead, focus on maintaining your balance. Be authentic, open, and transparent in any situation that comes your way. Rise above the noise, stay true to yourself and your values, and be kind and respectful toward those around you.

> *"When you change the way you look at things,*
> *the things you look at change." – Wayne Dyer*

We looked at visualization when we talked about triggers. Visualization is a useful exercise in many aspects of leadership: you can visualize future plans and successes before they ever happen or visualize your reactions to possible situations and see yourself rise above them as the leader you want to be.

In some circumstances, you may have to recalibrate a situation in order to rise above it. Recalibration can become necessary in relationships, but also in expectations and in your interpretation of a situation. Viewing something from another person's perspective can help you recalibrate your response. *Be willing to see things through the lens of others.* Appreciate and practice empathy.

Seek to create sustainability. Through your agility, focus, and effectiveness, you can develop your leadership skills and maintain equilibrium throughout any of the changes that come your way. Learn to ride the wave. Master change and enjoy the process.

Stability

We have gone over the concept of *riding the wave* and why it's so critical. Navigating stormy waters requires stability. In our world of intense and constant change, your people need you to be stable, and demonstrate strength, resilience, and confidence in overcoming challenges and hurdles to reach the heights of success and greatness. If you don't believe it and demonstrate it, you cannot expect your people to.

Stability is incredibly important in being an Agile Leader and creating a *safe work environment* where people are confident, and believe in themselves and in their teams, in their ability to move quickly and decisively, and in their potential to succeed. Your team will feel they are on stable ground if they know how you typically and consistently handle most situations.

Leading in Difficult Times

Whether your company is going through a business transformation or a major crisis, *leaders need to lead*. You often don't see the change coming and may not be prepared. But when a crisis occurs, it's time to unify your team and do what you can to help those around you with the difficult and important decisions that must be made. What are the steps leaders take during a crisis to pivot focus, create a successful mindset, establish clear communication, and step up? When there is a crisis, how can you become a more agile leader, team, and organization?

Here are a few suggestions.

Support others. During times of uncertainty, many leaders fail to support each other. You must recognize and resist this temptation, as it's easy to point fingers and jockey for position. Support your people, peers, and other leaders who need guidance and assistance. It's critical not to bury yourself in your office. You need to remain externally focused, so you can anticipate and pivot quickly when needed.

Be authentic. Be who you are. Continue to demonstrate the values, qualities, talents, and experiences that people already appreciate about you. Understand how others see and perceive you as a leader. Become more self-aware to understand how you and the messages you are sending are impacting others. Ask for feedback and input on your approach, how you communicate, and how you are leading.

Create stability. People need stability from you during times of chaos. Keep your managers close to their people, customers, and the marketplace. Have them continue to focus on daily tasks and deliverables. Encourage people to generate innovative ideas and to challenge the status quo. A team that feels safe is willing to take risks to achieve more and think differently, even through tough times.

Build trust. Trust your people with their decisions, actions, and responsibilities. Relationships need to be cultivated, and a downturn is the worst possible time to slash leadership and team-building budgets, if avoidable. People will hold you accountable to what you say and do, and what they *believe* you mean or do.

Communicate. When you are in the middle of a firestorm, it's easy to want to rush out with information. Slow things down. At the same time, communicate clearly, concisely, openly, and frequently. When there's a void of information, people will create their own story. The story they create can be significantly worse than reality.

Stay true to your core. Your purpose, mission, and values are more important than ever and should be the north star that guides your decision making. Your actions and your organization's actions should reflect these. Making purposeful decisions based on the company's mission and values will motivate teams to work toward a common goal. This is a good time to reflect on your organization's mission and purpose.

Lead with compassion. You may know what your company needs, but do you know what your people need? Take the time to really listen to your people and be empathetic. Show them you care about their perspectives. Let their insights play a role in your decision making, so they feel heard, and recognize that people have different coping mechanisms to handle pressure, stress, and anxiety.

Prioritize your wellbeing. As we discussed in chapter 7 regarding triggers, manage your emotions, and stay calm. Anticipate the unexpected during uncertain and unpredictable times. Modeling negativity, erratic behavior, and a lack of composure will cause your people to internalize and mimic this to others. Ensure you're prioritizing your mental and physical health so you can be present and effective.

Be the example. As a leader, you often forget that all eyes are on you. This is especially true as situations escalate. In such moments, people look to you, evaluating your words, actions, and body language for interpretation and direction. Be confident, positive, optimistic, and demonstrate what's possible. Think of an emergency room of nurses and doctors trying to save a patient.

Let go. During significant turbulence, some leaders tend to assert control, taking away their people's decision-making responsibilities to minimize risk. Ensure that the hierarchy and your need to control don't stifle the emergence of the best people with the best ideas. Talent will reveal itself during a crisis, and the strongest leadership will come from those with and without leadership titles. Don't stand in the way of the "stars in the making" that can emerge.

Create alignment. When the senior team is not aligned, it reverberates throughout the organization. Gain alignment on a shared vision, strategy, talent, and culture relative to how you will execute. Be able to describe what success looks like. Who will be accountable and responsible for what? What's the plan? How will you get there? Be flexible, agile, and prepared to pivot when needed.

Be tough. Being a tough leader means making hard decisions, coping with adversity, and demanding top performance from employees. There's no shame in getting knocked down—and it will happen, especially during a difficult time. What matters is what you do next. Get back into the game and keep fighting. That requires resilience, an ability to flex with adversity, and perseverance when the going gets rough.

Be decisive. People will expect actions and decisions from you. You want to avoid analysis paralysis. Entrust experts if and when needed. Assimilate the information, ask for recommendations and counsel, then listen to your instincts and experiences to make a decision.

Protect the culture. Focus on your culture, people, and values. Challenge yourself and your team on what needs to change about your culture to address your needs of the future. *Keep faith in the future.*

Leading in difficult times requires courage, emotional intelligence, and integrity. Be humble and prepared, and don't panic. Be resolute in pursuing the principles you believe are right, even in the face of opposition.

Addressing Accidental Leadership

When riding the wave, you don't just show up and try to wing it—bad things can happen. I will never forget the first time I rode the Pan-Mass Challenge (PMC), an annual distance biking event that raises money to fight for a cure of cancer. It was 1994 and I was in good shape and confident in my abilities. I borrowed a bike from a friend and proceeded to ride the 194-mile ride in two days—with *many* hills. I didn't train at all and when I was done, it took me two weeks to recover! I was a mess. Looking back, what was I thinking? A good lesson learned about not trying to wing it.

According to a recent presentation from the Center for Creative Leadership, 60% of managers say they have never received management training and 50% are rated as ineffective. Are these factors related? It seems likely that they are.[15]

Are you in a management role now? Do you have new managers working for you? How did you get there? How did they get there? Were you or they trained or prepared for the management position, or are you or they what we call an *accidental leader*?

Perhaps your (or their) rise to management looked something like this: You were doing your job and doing it well—maybe exceptionally well. You may have been making a lot of money for your company through your results, thought leadership and/or expertise.

---

[15] William A. Gentry et al., "Understanding the Leadership Challenges of First-Time Managers: Strengthening Your Leadership Pipeline," Center for Creative Leadership, 2015

Then one day, someone tapped you on the shoulder and offered you a management position.

There are many attractive reasons to move into management: an increase in salary, greater influence in the company, the prospect of respect and admiration from peers and the marketplace, and the hopeful promise of greater advances in the future. Drawn by some or all of these possibilities, you left your successful position and entered the management track.

Now what?

Maybe you were born for management and naturally thrive in it or have worked incredibly hard at it through self-learning and some mentorship. Or, do you find yourself serving as a glorified babysitter for a group of co-workers who were once your peers, but may now resent your new position? Or worse, do you feel you have to start over and wipe out the team below you so you can hire "your own people?"

With no training on how to deal with interpersonal relationships or managing and leading a team, you flounder along, trying to do your best in a difficult environment. Eventually, you may get frustrated, burnt out, or leave the organization. This happens far too often in companies that don't invest in training and developing their managers.

Accidental leaders account for a number of people in organizational management. They are often high achievers or top producers in the jobs they were hired to do. Then, suddenly, they are thrust into management. Logic says that people who are good at what they do should be able to manage others to do the same. While this certainly can be true, and there are many examples of managers who have been successful in this path, it is unlikely to work in the long term without the right management training and leadership development. As a result, these managers often fail. Or, if they don't fail entirely, they limp through a lackluster career in middle management, doing the best they can, but ultimately proving to be ineffective.

Too many employees are managed by people at this level. They continue a cycle of being hired for jobs and promoted if they're good at their jobs, without being properly developed. This is a huge risk for organizations. It impacts productivity, engagement, your culture, your ability to retain top talent, and ultimately, profits. As we saw earlier, an unengaged workforce is costly.

This doesn't have to be your fate, or the fate of your managers or organization. Although there are companies that continue to follow this ineffective mode of promoting top performers into management, there are better ways to operate. Some organizations now offer an individual performance career track, in which employees can continue to excel at what they do best, whether that means increasing and honing their skills to improve results or becoming experts in their fields. A few companies have realized the need for better management training and leadership development and offer their employees the chance to learn the necessary people skills and core competencies of effective management and leadership. And of course, there are courses and books, like this, that offer individuals the opportunity to take control of their own skills and learn the framework for great leadership.

If you are an *accidental leader*, or have them working for you, what can you do?

Acknowledge where you or they are in the journey. Check your/ their attitude. Then, work on necessary skills.

Whether you're an *accidental leader* or management has been in your sights since you started, you can improve your skills and techniques to position yourself to lead your people and your company to new heights.

Insights from Sports Management

Perhaps the biggest exception to the management rule in which the stars become the leader, is sports. In any sport, the best athletes become the starters and the stars. But they rarely become coaches. Most of the coaches and managers of sports teams were athletes at some point, and none of them were the stars.

Let's take one of the best managers in baseball history, Tommy Lasorda. He played in the minor leagues for a few years and played for the Dodgers for two seasons, but not as a star player—he mostly played in the farm system. But Lasorda went on to manage the Dodgers for 20 years and is in the Baseball Hall of Fame as a manager. He was never a star player, but he was an excellent manager. He won eight division titles, four National League pennants, and two World Series championships during his 20-year career. Lasorda is famous for his optimism and enthusiasm. As an example of just how powerful self-confidence can be, Lasorda's teams often overachieved thanks to his relentless optimism. Lasorda preached every day; you've got to believe! In his words, "I said it because I believed it, and I wanted my players to believe it."

Lasorda's mantra and belief are that winning isn't about being the best, but believing you are the best. He maintained that it's not always the strongest person who wins the fight, or the fastest person who wins the race, it's who wants it more.

He famously once said that managing is like holding a dove in your hand: if you hold it too tightly, you kill it, but if you hold it too loosely, you lose it. The most effective bosses are in tune with their people enough to know when to push and when to back off.

Self-confidence is the first step towards success. Lasorda was a masterful influencer and inspired many to achieve beyond what they believed they could. He never wavered in his passion, positivity, support, and belief in his teams. He would never let himself, a team member, or the team compromise his expectations.

Confidence determines how hard you will work and how high you will climb. If you don't believe you can do something, why would you work hard at it? If you don't truly believe your dreams can come true, why chase them?

Great leaders know how important confidence is in determining results. It sets the tone for everything that follows.

If you look at all sports, their best athletes rarely, if ever, became managers. Yet in the corporate and non-profit world, your star performers are the ones who usually become managers. There are exceptions to this, but the natural tendency for organizations is to make the top performer or expert into the next manager.

Entrepreneurs and Leadership

Perhaps your path to leadership was different. You forged your own path and are an entrepreneur. Successful entrepreneurs share similar qualities: they are visionary, passionate, tenacious, unafraid of failure or risk, curious, opportunistic, flexible, and ready to challenge the world around them.

It takes a person with conviction and resourcefulness to start a new business and manage it effectively through its infancy and initial growth. Entrepreneurs are undaunted by failures and mistakes and can pick themselves up off the ground. They demonstrate resilience and focus and constantly challenge the status quo.

It takes a brave person to become an entrepreneur and an even braver one to become both an entrepreneur and a leader. As a company grows and matures, so too must the management capability and effectiveness of its founder. There is only so much one person can do. Growth slows when there are few, if any, decisions being made that they are not intimately involved in. They need to delegate decisions and authority.

At some point, every entrepreneur must be willing to let go of the reins and share the responsibility and authority of management. There needs to be a clear definition of the next phase of vision and mission articulated for all to understand; an entrepreneur has to identify, surround themselves with, and develop a strong team.

The shift of being a pure entrepreneur to being a leader and entrepreneur is significant, requiring a different mindset, skill set, and level of agility. Do yourself a favor and hire an executive coach to help you with this transition. As we know, asking for help is a sign of strength, not weakness. As you go through several phases of your business growth cycle, you want to develop the skills and attributes necessary to continue to lead and build the business you started.

Coaching Entrepreneurs

Executive coaching enables entrepreneurs to tackle difficult topics and become a better version of themselves.

Coaching holds you accountable. An executive coach helps you set clear goals and take action, holding you accountable to what you say you want to achieve. Your executive coach works with you to understand why you choose certain actions, which helps you develop more self-awareness and mindfulness as a leader. An executive coach wants to ensure you're showing up to work and life the way you intend to.

Coaching challenges you. You get to a point in your life where no one really challenges you. Who is going to push you to push yourself? Who is going to give you honest feedback? Mentors and advisors will help, but often only to the extent that it relates to your business. An executive coach is a partner in crime and a mirror, saying things like, "This is how I see you being right now…" or, "What I'm hearing is…" to help you see how you're coming across to others. They will push you to truly understand your values, know your default reactive behaviors, embrace your strengths, and trust your instincts.

Coaching creates a safe and confidential space. There's so much pressure—externally, internally, and self-imposed—to do well. You may feel the need to conceal weaknesses or hesitate in openly discussing failures or worries, which can lead you to tipping points of frustration and exhaustion. You need to have someone to help you work on yourself. You may wrestle being honest and open about your struggles with mentors and advisors. Contrarily, an executive coach is neutral, creating a transparent environment to talk through difficult circumstances, reminding you to focus on your priorities, help you build up resilience, and most importantly ask, "Are you taking care of yourself?"

Executive coaching is about getting you to your peak performance. Once you've been coached, a certain part of you becomes a coach. As a leader, this is a powerful gift to help your colleagues or employees help themselves, ultimately improving your business and your bottom line.

A Harvard Business Review study on leadership shows the single unifying characteristic of a leader is their commitment to self-development.[16] Outstanding leaders are always learning more about themselves; working to get out of their own way and increase their performance. And just like on a sports team, a coach can play a pivotal role.

---

[16] Bill George, Peter Sims, Andrew N. McLean, Diana Mayer, "Discovering Your Authentic Leadership, " Harvard Business Review, February 2007

Ask yourself—do you want to play a bigger game? What is the single biggest thing holding you back? Let an executive coach help you go from great to exceptional.

Chapter 15: Purpose

As you progress in leadership, you will need to develop a certain presence. The ability to own a room, influence large groups of people, and command attention is often referred to as *executive presence*. Successful leaders have it. People who run organizations have it. And the good news is, anyone can develop it.

Belief

Believe in yourself, in your people, and your strategy. *Belief* is powerful.

In business, you are almost always trying to convince, educate, persuade, or influence someone about something — and it might not always be a product. It can be your ideas, your mission, your passion, or your purpose. Whatever it is, if you don't believe in it yourself, how can you influence others? You have to believe in where you're going and how you'll get there. You don't have to be extroverted or enthusiastic to inspire people. Show confidence. Hiring managers hire people they like and who have confidence. Not arrogance, but contagious confidence.

People are drawn to those who demonstrate belief in their vision. People want to be around those who exude confidence in their ability to have an impact, make a difference, and reach desired outcomes. Confident belief is magnetic. Belief is not arrogance, or narcissism, *it's unwavering faith.*

It is essential to have someone in your life who believes in you, who is looking out for you, and who has your back. Look back on your life and think of someone who believed in you, whether it was a friend, parent, teacher, or another person of influence. Now think about how that helped you overcome your obstacles. How powerful was that to you? How powerful can that be for you to give to others?

As leaders, when we demonstrate belief in people, it has that same power. Your belief can propel someone to a whole new level.

Purpose

What is your *purpose*?

> *"The two most important days in your life are the day you are born, and the day you find out why."*
> –Mark Twain

We wish it were that easy! Trying to find out who we are and what our purpose is in life is just not that easy. For most of us, life is an uneven journey with unexpected twists, turns, and side roads; a journey of discovering what we want, what we're good at, and what's important to us. Depending on where we are in life, priorities will vary, and our perspective will change depending on the experiences, successes, and failures we have or don't have.

So, how do we navigate effectively? How do we determine our purpose in career, leadership, and life? Here is a short list of important reminders as we reflect on our quest to find purpose:

- Be curious.
- Don't set limitations; continue to challenge yourself.
- Be ok with failing and learning.
- Be resilient, accept change, and demonstrate grit.
- Identify your passion.
- Understand and accept yourself and others.
- Be humble and authentic.
- Learn from others.
- Admit what you don't know and when you made a mistake.

Your purpose is who you are and what makes you unique; it's your brand, what you're driven to achieve, the essence of what makes you tick, and the impact you will have on the world around you. Your purpose needs to resonate with you. Think about what that means. What energizes you? What brings you immense gratification? What are the experiences and moments that have shaped you and now motivate you? Write down a few ideas; discuss it with someone close to you. It might be right in front of you, or you are already searching for what it could be. How will you live your purpose and impact others? How will you help people find their passion, their purpose? If you want to become an exceptional leader, you have to know your purpose and be able to help people find theirs.

Using Purpose to Unleash Your Full Potential

As a business, are you advocating your purpose rather than products or services? While employees and consumers might turn to a brand for its products or solutions, they stick around for the company's mission, its purpose on why it exists, and what they aspire to become.

Consider the consumer's experience. What will your client's or consumer's experience be with your product or service? Starbucks used to say that they were not in the coffee business, that they were in business to provide their customers a "home away from their home" experience. Harley Davidson's position was that they were not in the motorcycle business, they were in the "freedom on the road" business. What is the experience you are providing?

A generation ago, most people didn't consider what a company stood for when making a purchase or accepting a job offer. But today, consumers and job candidates want to know. How will you answer them?

While all generations are asking this question, millennials and younger generations prioritize purpose. Business leaders are taking notice, perhaps because Pew Research Center reported that 75% of the workforce will be made up of millennials by 2025—with many millennials now holding leadership positions. Research from Cone Communications, meanwhile, found that 64% of millennials wouldn't accept a job at a company that they didn't see as having strong corporate social responsibility values.

Businesses that want to build high-performing teams and compete in the 21st century must pay attention to what this research suggests. Tech-savvy consumers and candidates can quickly identify and learn about companies whose ideals match their own. It's a fascinating development that won't end any time soon, because Generation Z, hot on the heels of millennials, is following suit.

How do you make your company's purpose stick?

Purpose and profit can coexist. Start to create alignment by ensuring that your *why* (your purpose) and your *how* (your operations) are in sync. The Patagonia story is a perfect example of how purpose and profit aligned successfully. In 2011, the company ran a full-page ad in the *New York Times* on Black Friday with a simple statement: "Don't Buy This Jacket." The advertisement featured the company's best-selling R2 jacket with a clear message against consumerism: "The environmental cost of everything we make is astonishing." The ad continued, "There is much to be done and plenty for us all to do. Don't buy what you don't need. Think twice before you buy anything."

It sounded risky, but the strategy worked. According to an article about this campaign in Entrepreneur Magazine, Patagonia experienced record-breaking sales of $10 million—five times higher than expected. Then, Patagonia donated profits to charitable organizations in support of environmental causes.

As a leader, part of your role is to inspire others to follow you. Giving your employees and customers a sense of purpose, of participating in something bigger, is one way to accomplish that. That means leading by example and reminding everyone of the "why." It must go beyond receiving a paycheck and great health benefits — that kind of benefit can only get you so far with your employees.

When you run an organization, you need to have a purpose. This goes deeper than goals or objectives; it's about the reasons why you do what you do; what you aspire to be. Direction, strategy, and goals can change, but your purpose is your identity, who you are, who you are trying to become. Whether you're running a company, or a department or a shift, you have to clarify your purpose and communicate to others how they need to behave, operate, and communicate to live and achieve that purpose.

Endurance and Resilience

Agile leadership requires the ability to endure. Failure is part of growth, and it is one of the most painful parts. Many people are tempted to give up when they fail. But those who succeed are able to push through failure, endure the pain, and achieve success. There has been research, writing, and TED Talks about the one differentiator of students, professionals, and leaders who thrive and overcome obstacles regardless of background, disadvantages, or advantages. It's *grit*. Grit is the blend of passion, perseverance, purpose, optimism, and effort. It's focus and energy towards your goals, even in the face of adversity. It's picking yourself up, time after time, and not giving up.

Many famous leaders failed more than once on the way to success. Bill Gates dropped out of college before he built Microsoft. He also failed many other times before getting it right. There is a level of resilience or endurance that comes with being a leader. You have to learn how to overcome obstacles, to deal with doubt and fear.

How do you overcome these obstacles? It's a powerful characteristic that many leaders have, an unwavering belief in themselves that helps them overcome doubt and failure. It requires purpose and knowledge of what they're out to accomplish in the world.

There are many examples throughout history of people from many countries, cultures, and backgrounds who overcame great obstacles on the way to success. How did they do it? These people have inner belief and drive that they can overcome; a vision of what they want to do, plus the strength and endurance to accomplish it.

Multiple Generations

There are more generations in the workforce than ever. Baby Boomers, Gen X, Millennials, and Gen Z are all currently holding jobs and shaping companies. This creates more complexity in workplace dynamics.

Younger generations use technology differently, communicate differently, and have different ideas of career and life success. Instead of a traditional career ladder, they view career success more holistically: they often aren't openly interested in leadership. Instead, they take on more informal leadership roles, moving naturally into what fits them best.

This tendency of younger generations is becoming more prevalent in organizations: they don't want the pressure and stress of leadership; they don't just want vacations, they want sabbaticals; they're more interested than older generations in the environment and social issues, as well as true work/life balance. They look at their parents—how hard they worked and how little free time they had—and they don't necessarily want to work more hours to get more.

Formal leadership is all about titles, while informal leadership is more about influence. Informal leaders don't need the title to have a significant impact and influence on others. Leaders have to be aware of who their key influencers are, regardless of title.

Every new generation is different from the one that came before. You can't categorize or stereotype a whole generation, but there are notable differences. Leaders have to understand the motivations and needs of different generations, as well as the different cultures and personalities of each individual.

Managing a Remote Workforce

There are more remote teams today than ever before and the shift to remote work is having a positive impact. In the last 10 years the remote workforce has grown 149%, and 85% of businesses confirm that productivity has increased in their company due to greater flexibility. Additionally, 90% of employees say allowing for more flexible work arrangements and schedules would_increase morale, while 77% say allowing employees to work remotely may lead to lower operating costs.[17]

The definition of a remote worker and/or team continues to change and evolve, as do the conditions that necessitate it. Various factors have contributed to the increase in remote work, including globalization, shifts in technology, the ability to attract top talent, and cost and productivity effectiveness. Uncontrollable situations, such as a natural disaster or public health crisis, can also cause companies to adopt remote work.

Whether you are managing a global team with members in different countries and time zones, a team whose interactions are impacted by travel or preferred work schedule, or a team that works

---

[17] Beth Braccio Hering, Remote Work Statistics: Shifting Norms and Expectations, FlexJobs.com, February 2020

in different offices/locations, how you manage the work and lead your people needs to be different from an in-office approach.

Working remotely, when managed properly, can be a time and cost savings to an organization, providing flexibility to your people, which can boost their morale. But when managed improperly, it can harm an organization's productivity, effectiveness, and culture. Technology has made it easier to manage a team or workforce virtually, but there are still challenges.

Communicating a shift to remote work. Whether this was a shift you were planning for, are utilizing occasionally, or are now rapidly adopting as a reaction to something, the first step should always be clear communication from leadership. Working from home could last a week, several months, or become a permanent strategy for some or all of your workforce. Take advantage of this moment to better equip your team or organization to work remotely for the long term. Communicate to teams or organization-wide and provide employees a training session (virtually, if needed) on how to work remotely and best practices for working with others virtually.

Before you communicate and train, gather feedback and collect data from employees who are already working remotely, along with managers. What works, and what hasn't been working? What are the lessons learned and best practices? You should reach out to other organizations who have had experiences with remote workforces to get their insights as well.

During any period of transition, your team will look to managers and key influencers for guidance and support. Make sure they are equipped to provide best practices and strategies. Get them on board and excited. Develop them to be able to manage a remote workforce, to help drive new behaviors within the organization, and to lead the change.

To be successful, every team member has to get comfortable with a new paradigm, set of tools, processes, and methods to be productive *as individuals and as a team.* Because this change ultimately impacts how your team works together, which has implications for how each individual works, it's vital that they understand that this is about rethinking the way that they operate so that remote work can be just as productive and fulfilling as collaborating in person. When any one person fails to adopt these new ways of working, it becomes far more evident than in a traditional environment.

Understand your remote employees. As a remote leader, you likely don't get a chance to spend much time interacting with your employees and discovering what makes them tick. While it's possible to learn what drives your employees over time, an accelerator may be more useful. For remote leaders, I recommend a workplace behavioral assessment—such as the PI Behavioral Assessment—to give you a wealth of information about your employees' drivers, needs, and natural work styles. It will help you understand how they like to work, interact and be rewarded. For example, if you know someone has a low degree of extraversion, it might be okay to contact them infrequently, but ensure they are staying connected to others and not secluding themselves. On the other hand, if an employee has high extraversion, you might want to spend more time interacting with them and providing facetime, as they need to be connected.

Put more of an emphasis on managing. While co-located teams often benefit most from an in-person manager, remote teams need a manager who provides clearly defined direction and removes all ambiguity from the process. When a team works together in the same office, you can have loose job descriptions, possibly even with two people sharing elements of the same role. With remote teams, managers need to define roles and responsibilities—starting with their own. They also need a strong process by which to clarify and track commitments, progress, and deliverables.

Don't be a helicopter boss. Each person on your team has a different rhythm and workflow. Don't micromanage it. A huge key to the success of remote teams is trust—trust that your employees are doing their job, even if their workflow isn't the same as yours. Of course, if an employee has abused that trust, a different conversation must take place.

This means not using little check-in tricks to see if they're working or not early in the morning or throughout the day. These types of "gotchas" destroy trust and create ambiguity.

Set clear expectations. Remote employees need a healthy dose of trust—even when they are doing things their way. However, this doesn't mean they're running the show. It's important to set and communicate clear expectations about how you'll judge their work performance and any practices, guidelines, or updates you, as a manager, need to see. For example, if starting working by 8:30 a.m. is non-negotiable for you or if you really need people to tell you when they'll be away from their desks longer than an hour, it needs to be communicated clearly from the outset. Ensure that you delegate work, empower team members to make decisions, and monitor progress.

Invite constructive feedback. Despite the lack of regular face-to-face interaction, create a two-way dialogue such that team members feel comfortable providing constructive feedback to each other and to you that will enhance your and the team's effectiveness and transparency.

Build relationships differently. Relationships take on a whole new meaning in remote teams. When you meet your colleagues by the "water cooler" or coffee shop every day, you develop informal relationships with them; they tend to form more naturally. In a remote team, you need to create situations where interactions occur, "meeting" regularly. Informal meetings should be done both online—through videoconferencing—and face-to-face. Depending on the state of the team, business, and market, meeting remotely should be done every week or once every few weeks. In-person meetings, if plausible, should be done at least twice a year. Even if companies are cutting costs, this is a cost well spent on building relationships, gaining alignment, and strengthening your culture.

You can also encourage groups to meet up for a monthly coffee hour, dinner, or other activity on their own time. These are not company events and cost the company nothing but continue to foster culture. Because teammates don't see each other every day in the traditional sense, we have noticed that these events generally get a high turnout and people really enjoy the non-work related interactions.

Communicate differently. Remote employees still need clarity, communication, and connectedness. To keep them engaged, it's important to build in frequent weekly meetings, including one-on-ones, team check-ins, and more. Encourage your remote team members to also have one-on-ones with each other at least every couple of weeks. This will help keep them "in the know," as well as build rapport. Share information in a timely manner by establishing informal and formal communication vehicles to keep team members informed and engaged.

Create guidelines that establish norms of behavior when participating in remote meetings, such as limiting background noise and side conversations, talking clearly and at a reasonable pace, listening attentively, not dominating the conversation, and so on. You should include preferences about which communication modes to use in which circumstances, for example, when to reply via email versus picking up the phone versus taking the time to create and share a document.

Make video communication an essential. The first crucial step in a strong remote work culture is having the team adopt and commit to using videoconferencing. Although this may seem like a "nice to have" feature, it's a critical factor for remote work success. Human beings, ultimately, feel more connected when we can see each other. Most of how we communicate comes through our body language, eye contact, and other forms of nonverbal communication.

I have found that in today's hyper-connected world that many employees and managers struggle to refrain from multitasking when not on a video. It's easy to become distracted and let your attention drift when others can't see you. This can be an issue with remote development and learning as well. Being on camera typically makes team members more present, which ultimately leads to more effective communication, retention, productivity, and actionable next steps.

A challenge to remote work being effective and widely adopted can be thrown off by team members struggling with technology issues. Make sure every team member has high-speed internet access, a functional webcam, and a good microphone and headset. Everyone should be using a headset with a noise-canceling microphone to avoid echoing, feedback loops, or muffled audio that can cause any meeting to break down. We've all had that experience and know how frustrating and distracting it can be, to the point where it can shut down a meeting and productivity entirely.

For group meetings, require that all attendees, if possible, join via video. This helps everyone feel connected, but most importantly, it shows that people are mentally present and focused. Make sure everyone understands how to screen-share and, when relevant, share collaborative documents with team members in the meeting. Being able to work on one document as a group is efficient and effective. If some team members can't attend, share a recording of the meeting in a relevant channel for others to review later.

These are simple acts that require little or no effort once you learn to adopt the tools that make a significant difference for collaborative teams.

I have found that most meetings can be completed in 30 minutes and that dropping the length of the meetings gets all participants more focused on achieving an outcome in the allotted time. Since you may need to connect with more people virtually during the day, these shorter, more focused meetings leave more time to execute tasks or have quick check-ins with other team members, if needed.

I recommend focusing on *"working sessions"* versus meetings when possible. Some meetings are designed to share information and bring consensus. Still, when working with colleagues to complete tasks, I find it's very productive to bring multiple team members together to sit in a virtual meeting where we all work on our respective tasks to complete a broader initiative. Just knowing that you can quickly discuss things in real-time while all working on the same collaborative document can force entire teams to rally towards completing a project faster on a tighter deadline. It's also a fun way to interact with colleagues that fosters a deeper collaborative culture.

Practice over-communication. In a remote work environment, it is not unusual for employees or managers to question another person's productivity if they don't have visibility into their activities. That's why I stress that remote employees need to be over-communicative in letting their peers and managers understand their output. For some employees, being vocal and drawing attention to themselves is uncomfortable, but in a remote working environment, it's key that employees push through this feeling and make sure that their managers and their peers understand what they're working on. Over-communication may ensure that everyone on the team is confident that each team member is productive and working in the same direction, and an additional byproduct is that collaboration and productivity increase.

Another effective practice that can help, especially in fast-moving organizations, is a daily *"stand-up."* This concept is taken from scrum software development but can be useful in any organization. It requires that each team member "stand-up" and share what work they completed since the last meeting, what they're actively focused on, and if they have any impediments to completing those tasks. By nature, over-communication and the concept of doing a "stand-up" are aligned to delivering outcomes and holding people accountable to their own word. Documenting actions, progress, and deliverables also keeps people on track and accountable.

The downside of remote work. Pay attention to how your people may struggle with being alone, managing their family dynamics at home, or dealing with stress and anxiety. Others may have a difficult time stopping work and giving themselves adequate breaks during the day.

Onboarding a new hire remotely becomes a challenge in acclimating them to your culture. A new hire will face challenges in developing relationships with their new team and in their ability to become acclimated with processes and systems everyone else takes for granted.

It becomes more challenging to be visible and to build relationships and connections with other key people in the company and leadership. The lack of visibility can impact potential promotions and advancement opportunities.

Build a remote and virtual work culture. When implementing a remote workforce, focus on over-communication, boundaries, and protocols of how to work together, and establishing relationships and trust. It's critical to establish trust among employees, pride in their work, and a shared sense of accountability and accomplishment. We find that team members build strong personal relationships by collaborating. They have increased respect for and deeper understanding of their co-workers as a result of over-communication, high levels of interpersonal interactions, and shared values and standards.

Remote work gives team members more time for themselves, their loved ones, and their hobbies, which helps people deal with the stresses of work in a more productive manner. Healthy, happy, and engaged team members tend to be more productive and more focused during their work hours. Most don't want to lose the privilege of working remotely and virtually and will make the extra effort to maintain that privilege.

It's also essential to learn the differences in managing a global remote team. You need to understand and respect cultural differences and nuances in developing relationships, communicating, assigning tasks, and forming effective teams.

Remote work can transform your business. Remote work works! Adopting the best practices of remote work will make your team better communicators and collaborators. Making every member of the team effective at working remotely makes teams more conscious of how to work with other online team members and even third-party partners or vendors.

Whether your company's future is 100% remote or some hybrid of onsite and remote, these practices will modernize your organization and make it more resilient to emergencies while minimizing risks to your company's productivity.

Developing the Next Generation of Leaders

While 86% of leaders believe leadership succession planning is an "urgent" or "important" priority, only 14% believe they do it well.[18]

Just 27% of business units have the leaders they need for the future![19]

Developing future leaders is critical for your organization. It's more than a legacy; it's about responsibility. Leaders should be asking, what am I doing to develop the next generation of leaders? What more could I do? Does my organization have an effective succession planning process and structure, and does it work? Are you a mentor to guide and influence? Are you being an advocate for those who have essential qualities for moving up into leadership? Always be on the lookout for someone you can develop.

Here is a simple exercise you can do in helping stretch and develop your leaders. For staff meetings, have each of your direct reports run the meeting. Rotate the responsibility to each of them and continue to include yourself. This becomes an effective way to see how your people prepare for the meeting, ask or not ask for input from others, how they run the meeting, facilitate dialogue (or not), identify action items and next steps, and resolve conflict. You will be able to observe, take notes, and debrief with each of them after.

---

[18] Adam Canwell et al., "Leaders at all levels: Close the gap between hype and readiness," Deloitte University Press, March 7, 2014.
[19] Gartner, Succession Plan for the Future

This is a wonderful development and coaching approach and helps you understand their strengths and development needs.

Mentorship and Advocacy

Earlier, I touched on the need for mentors and advocates in the process of developing leaders. This important aspect of leadership is often overlooked. Still, it is essential not only for your success but for the success of those who follow you.

Do you have a mentor? A mentor can be someone inside your organization or outside, either a personal or professional guide. If you don't have that person in your life, find someone. Many leaders have multiple people they can go to for help. Even the most successful leaders still don't know what they don't know. They still need advice, input, and encouragement.

Do you have an advocate? Someone on your side? An advocate is someone from within your organization who is advocating for you, keeping you in mind for projects, exposure, and promotions. Keep that in mind: an advocate will look out for you and support you as you advance in your career.

A mentor and advocate can be the same person but most likely are not. Advocates are not mentoring you but are advocating for you, where mentors are supporting, guiding, and providing advice and counsel.

Chapter 16: Emotional Intelligence

*"Whatever anybody says or does, assume
positive intent. You will be amazed at how
your whole approach to a person or problem
becomes very different." – Indra Nooyi*

Emotional intelligence ties into managing your emotions and self-awareness. It's part of the *two-sided coin* I described earlier, but it also involves being able to make decisions, guide teams and organizations, and give useful and constructive feedback. It is more than being a warm and kind person. It also involves being the kind of leader that people are willing to follow.

Leaders should have a high level of *emotional intelligence*. Evaluate yourself in this area, and ask others for feedback. Do you handle difficult people and situations with emotional maturity? Do you effectively manage your triggers? Can you cast a vision and forge ahead into new territory without leaving your people behind?

What Is Emotional Intelligence?

Emotional intelligence (EI) is the ability to understand and manage your own emotions, and those of the people around you. People with a high degree of emotional intelligence know what they're feeling, what their emotions mean, and how these emotions can affect other people.

For leaders, having emotional intelligence is essential for success. After all, who is more likely to succeed—a leader who shouts at his team when he's under stress, or a leader who stays in control and calmly assesses the situation to move forward to a solution?

According to Daniel Goleman, an American psychologist who helped to popularize EI, there are five main elements of emotional intelligence:

- Self-awareness
- Self-regulation
- Motivation
- Empathy
- Social skills

The more that you, as an Agile Leader, can manage each of these areas, the higher your emotional intelligence. So, let's look at each element in more detail and examine how you can grow as a leader.

Emotional Intelligence in Agile Leadership

Why does EI matter to leaders? As we have been discussing, today's leader must be agile. You must have the ability to shift your strategy and communicate differently based on the situation. *Situational awareness* is a skill that is closely linked with EI. Consider these statistics:

- 90% of top performers are high in EI.
- Just 20% of bottom performers are high in EI.[20]
- 70% of change initiatives fail because of:
  o People issues
  o Inability to lead and influence
  o Lack of teamwork
  o Unwillingness to take initiative, and inability to deal with change[21]

---

[20] Travis Bradberry, "Emotional Intelligence - EQ," Forbes, January 2014
[21] Carolyn Dewar and Scott Keller, "The Irrational Side of Change Management," McKinsey, April 2009

Let's look at each of the five components of EI in closer detail.

Self-Awareness

If you're self-aware, you know how you feel and how your emotions and actions can affect the people around you. Being self-aware in a leadership position also means having a clear picture of your strengths and weaknesses and behaving with humility. So, what can you do to improve your self-awareness?

Take the PI Behavioral Assessment. Take the PI Behavioral Assessment to learn about your strengths and potential derailers, especially under pressure and stress, what happens when you overuse your strengths, and what your natural management and leadership style is.

Keep a journal. If you spend just a few minutes each day writing down your thoughts, it can move you to a higher degree of self-awareness. Utilize the triggers exercise I provided earlier in the book.

Slow down. When you experience anger or other strong emotions, slow down to examine why. Remember, no matter what the situation, you can always choose how you react to it.

Self-Management

Leaders who manage themselves effectively rarely verbally attack others, make rushed or emotional decisions, stereotype people, or compromise their values. Self-regulation is all about staying in control and being *measured*. This is about a leader's commitment to *personal accountability*.

So, how can you improve your ability to self-regulate?

Know your values. Do you have a clear idea of where you absolutely will not compromise? Do you know what values are most important to you? Spend some time examining your "code of ethics." If you know what's most important to you, then you probably won't have to think twice when you face a moral or ethical decision—you'll make the right choice. How you respond to not compromising is just as critical to having those values and standards.

Hold yourself accountable. If you tend to blame others when something goes wrong, stop. Make a commitment to admit to your mistakes and to face the consequences, whatever they are. You'll probably sleep better at night, and you'll quickly earn the respect of those around you.

Practice being calm and measured. The next time you're in a challenging situation, be aware of how you act. Review your triggers list and how you will anticipate and manage your emotions; how you will pause and concentrate on what you will say and how you will say it. Think about your coping mechanisms, especially under pressure and stress. What will you do to stay centered and balanced? How will you keep your mind and emotions calm and measured?

Motivation

Think you can or think you can't
—either way you are correct. – Henry Ford

Motivation is driven by purpose and a desire to make a difference. To inspire employee motivation, leaders must share their vision. It's not enough to just be optimistic—you must give your team and organization something to be optimistic and confident about. Talk about where you have been, where you are, and where you are going. Share your plan for a brighter and better future, talk about the actions you and your team must take, and reiterate the reasons why you and they will be successful. Create a vision that inspires and rallies your team and organization.

Your most important weapon against pessimism is transferring your optimism and vision to others. Inspire your teams to believe they can succeed so they can inspire their teams to do the same. Utilize every opportunity available to transfer your optimism.

People are most energized when they are using their strengths for a purpose beyond themselves. When employees feel as though the work they do is playing an integral role in the overall success of the company and the world, they are motivated to work harder, to help each other, and to help the team and organization reach new heights.

Empathy

Leaders with empathy can put themselves in someone else's situation and understand their perspective. They help develop the people on their team, challenge others who are acting unfairly, give constructive feedback, and listen to those who need it. Being empathetic is also critical when working with and addressing conflict.

If you want to earn respect and loyalty from your team, then show them you care by being empathetic.

Put yourself in someone else's position. It's easy to support your own point of view. After all, it's yours. Take the time to look at situations from other people's lenses and perspectives.

Pay attention to body language. Perhaps when you listen to someone, you cross your arms, move your feet back and forth, or bite your lip. This body language tells others how you feel about a situation, and the message you're sending isn't positive. Learning to read body language can be a real asset in a leadership role because you'll be better able to determine how someone truly feels. This allows you to respond appropriately.

Respond to feelings. Proactively identify how people may be feeling in a particular situation. Demonstrate your awareness of their feelings. Awareness of their feelings doesn't mean you agree with how they feel or condone they feel that way. Acknowledging that their feelings exist is a display of empathy. Pay attention to your emotional reaction and ensure you don't get caught up with their emotions.

Social Skills

Leaders who have mastered social skills are great communicators. They're just as open to hearing bad news as good news, and they're experts at getting their team to support them and be excited about a new mission or project.

Leaders who have excellent social skills are also good at managing change and resolving conflicts diplomatically. They're rarely satisfied with leaving conflict or discussions unresolved and don't sit back and make everyone else do the work. They set an example with their behavior.

So, how can you build social skills?

Learn conflict resolution. Leaders must know how to resolve conflicts between their team members, customers, or vendors. Learning conflict resolution skills is vital if you want to succeed.

Improve your communication skills. How well do you communicate? Think honestly about how effective you are at helping your audience *understand* your message. Work to minimize the distractions or blockers that may cause your audience to translate your message differently than you intend. Remember, communication isn't useful unless the other person clearly understands it.

Learn how to praise others. As a leader, you can inspire the loyalty of your team by giving praise when it's earned. Learning how to praise and appreciate others is a fine art, but well worth the effort.

Manage Your Emotional Agility

There seems to be a belief that negative emotions should not be expressed in the workplace. This holds especially true for leaders, who are expected to project positivity, enthusiasm, and support at all times, or to present a demeanor without negative feelings, doubt, criticism, fear, or anger. The pressure to be only positive can be incredibly stressful for all of us, especially leaders. A study showed that 47% of entrepreneurs found "positivity" as the most important trait a leader can have.[22]

Being positive, inspirational, and supportive is necessary. Still, it would help if you were realistic when things are not going well. How will you address and respond to bad news?

Is it realistic or healthy to only be positive? Should you be walking around on eggshells? You need to be able to recognize your emotions, and yes, be more measured when you are triggered. But you can't be robotic; you need to show when you have emotions.

---

[22] Kat Boorgard, "Hundreds of entrepreneurs deemed one trait the most important for effective leaders," Business Insider, March 2017

People do need to know if you are angry, upset, unhappy, or disappointed. People do need to understand and see the difference between when things are going well and when they are not, and know where they stand without compromising respect, support, or empathy. Demonstrate negative emotions in an effective or measured way. If you are not sure what that looks like, solicit a colleague or a mentor.

I had a client that struggled with controlling and managing his emotions. We went through my triggers methodology and exercise, and it was transformational for him. He showed up as a different person and executive. However, he over-rotated. He was so determined to be more measured and manage his emotions that his people didn't know where he stood and whether he was unhappy or disappointed. We were able to work through it, but it's an important reminder not to overcorrect and to show genuine human emotion effectively and authentically.

Emotional agility is about recognizing your emotions, as discussed in chapter 7, and developing the ability to prepare, anticipate, and then manage how you show up in a variety of situations. It's also about being able to move on and let go without significant emotional residue.

Chapter 17: Your Executive Presence

Executive presence is the combination of being able to command a room and interact with others, whether it be with one person, a team, or a broader audience. Certain people can develop this presence more easily than others, but ultimately, it's a skill that can be learned.

You don't have to be an alpha or gregarious personality to command presence. Are you able to influence those around you? Can you pause and reflect and ask the right questions? Do you pace yourself, control your emotions, and use the right tempo? Are you prepared and confident in your subject and content? These are elements of executive presence.

Executive presence is having a leadership quality in how you come across, share information, ask questions, develop people, work with teams, and communicate mission, vision, and purpose. You don't have to be an extrovert or assertive person. Quiet leaders can have that executive presence. Perhaps you've met a few.

In addition to being able to command a room, executive presence means being able to own a stage. It's the ability to stand and confidently give a presentation or speech, a critical skill for becoming a great leader.

If you are not comfortable speaking to a group of people, they will know it. You can improve your ability by joining a speaker's network, hiring a coach, or take a do-it-yourself approach. You can record yourself on video giving practice speeches, and then evaluating the video and making adjustments.

Qualities of Executive Presence

People who have executive presence are terrific at consistently projecting the following qualities to their audience:

Candor: Honesty and transparency, through the willingness and skill to constructively tell it like it is.

Clarity: The ability to tell your story in an intuitive, clear, and compelling way.

Openness: Not prejudging; being willing to consider another's point of view.

Passion: The expression of commitment, motivation, and drive that shows people you believe in what you do, that you love what you do, and that you believe in others and what they do.

Poise: The look of control or balance; of pausing when you need to gather your thoughts; of not getting rattled when you are attacked, accused, or challenged.

Self-confidence: The air of assurance, such that others know you have strength and resolve, but not arrogance. To be humble with belief.

Sincerity: The conviction of believing in and meaning what you say, with empathy.

Thoughtfulness: Thinking something through or carefully considering something before responding.

Warmth: Being accessible to others and being interested in them.

Notice that these qualities have nothing to do with the content of the message. Instead, they have to do with how you position the content and tell your story. They're about how you engage with others. That's because over 80% of most communication is non-verbal! Your audience, whether it's an audience of one or one thousand, is relying on things you do outside the content of your message to make important decisions about the message and you. Like most people, you probably don't spend much time working on these non-content things. However, your audience spends most of its time evaluating them. This disconnect is why many people are perceived as not having much executive presence or even executive potential.

Executive presence is an art, like negotiation skills. It's about developing your *voice*. Finding your voice is a personal journey and must be refined and mastered over time through experimentation, failure, and repeated execution.

Steps to Increase Executive Presence

Developing the qualities of executive presence is easier for some people than others, but with some work, you can become highly effective.

Embrace your unique value. Do not go into meetings doubting your value. Prepare in advance; develop your unique perspective based on your individual, hard-won experiences, and developed expertise. Then walk in knowing you are an asset. Know that. Be humble and grateful to share your knowledge and experiences with others.

Be self-aware. Be aware of your body language. A killer pitch can be destroyed by lousy non-verbal communication. Don't slouch. Don't wave your arms about like you are drowning at sea. Stand upright and poised. Breathe slowly and regularly. Look people in the eyes and genuinely engage. Be calm and purposeful with your hand gestures. All of this engenders trust. You look like you can handle anything—and you can.

Think before you speak. Many people ramble on, especially when excited or in the middle of a debate, without much thought for whether they make sense, are saying anything useful, or are being repetitive. So, choose your words carefully. Think about your ultimate objectives to meet your needs. Don't hurry to deliver the message. Take your time, be deliberate, pace yourself, and say much less than you think you need to. As discussed, *ask questions, facilitate dialogue* more, and offer fewer opinions.

Use the power of silence. Silence is an incredibly powerful tool and should never be underestimated. However, most of us feel awkward with silence and are compelled to fill it. When you pause, it shows you are in command of your thoughts, are not afraid to reflect and slow down, and that you are not trying to rush through your topic or presentation. It also allows you to adjust what you want to say, or possibly even take on a new direction.

A well-chosen pause also allows the listener to digest your message. At the same time, you will enable yourself to assess your listeners' behavior. When you do that, you can tailor your words and actions accordingly.

Engage with your audience. Persuasive communication is far more than what you are delivering. You need to relate to and engage with others. You need to make the audience feel like they matter to you. You do this by asking questions, gathering feedback, listening to what your audience says, reading their verbal and nonverbal cues, and discerning the appropriate response.

Know your material. Know what you are talking about when presenting, providing an opinion, making a suggestion, or engaging in a debate or disagreement. Hold your ground but be receptive and open to other views. Listen to what others are saying and acknowledge their points of view. Be confident in your knowledge and expertise. Participate when you are in a discussion that isn't your area of expertise and offer helpful questions and viewpoints. Be comfortable with what you know and don't know.

Utilize wit. Never forget your sense of humor. I've often heard leaders say they are afraid to use humor at the senior level in case they aren't taken seriously. Yet this can backfire, as people who take themselves too seriously are ironically taken less seriously by their peers. A study by *Bell Leadership Institute* found that the two most desirable traits in leaders were a strong work ethic and a good sense of humor. At the same time, be careful about how you use humor. Overly dry or sarcastic humor that cuts into someone or that few understand or appreciate isn't effective.

Humor is also vital to diffuse tension, as well-placed humor can diffuse an escalation or rising conflict.

Your originality sits at the core of your ability to communicate authentically and powerfully. So, continually nurture and refine yourself, your voice, and your inner strength.

Tell Your Story

You have to be able to tell your story, your *why*, your passion, and your purpose. People want to hear stories, stories that capture their hearts, dreams, and aspirations.

What is your story? Be open about the experiences that shaped you. Tell your compelling story of why you do what you do and how it has impacted you or others. You can tell a story of what you witnessed, or what was passed on to you that has affected you. You may have more than one story to demonstrate the various experiences and lessons you want to share. Claiming and sharing your history, or of others, will help you be comfortable being authentic and transparent. Telling your story helps with connection. It helps people relate. It establishes trust.

Take some time to think through these questions:

- How do you describe your story?
- Why are you where you are?
- How have you arrived there?
- Why do you do what you do?
- What led you there?
- What were your successes and failures along the way?
- What is your inspiration for what you do now?
- Why you?
- What inspires you?

Sometimes you have to share this with a colleague, a mentee, a team, or your organization, or perhaps at a talk or convention. Know your story. Tell it. Write it down and practice it. Fine-tune it for different audiences and different times in your life. Revisit it.

A story allows people to see you in a more in-depth manner. I had a client who struggled with relationships and with being open about himself. He was very private and reserved. We worked on his ability to connect, including with broader audiences. He incorporated stories about his personal experiences into his messages and presentations, not just as a professional but as a person. The impact was powerful: his brand and authenticity rocketed, as did his ability to connect with people he hardly knew. This gave him the confidence to become more comfortable in being open with his colleagues. As a result, he was able to establish stronger relationships and trust.

Your story will evolve, especially as you learn how to share it in ways that resonate most with others. Ultimately, this skill will become a powerful part of your presence and your authentic and transparent self.

Chapter 18: Be Strategic

"Failing to plan is planning to fail." – Anonymous

Strategy without planning and execution is just a good idea. As a manager who is aspiring to be a leader throughout your career, you need to pay attention to what it means to be strategic, regardless of your function, role, or level. Being strategic can be applied to operations, process, finance, technology, or externally focused marketing, or sales. Demonstrating you have strategic capability before it is required allows you to be considered for advancement. For example, if you are looking to move into a C-level role, you need to demonstrate that you are equipped with the capability to perform today. Leaders are not promoted for potential; they are promoted for demonstrating they can perform at that next level now.

Create time to think, plan, research, and to connect with others. I've seen too many managers running from meeting to meeting every day. Or worse, they try to create time to think or plan when they are at home with their families or on vacation. It doesn't work. Create time each week to think, research, and be externally focused; to speak and meet with people throughout the enterprise, clients, and people in the marketplace. You need to be continually recalibrating and assessing your goals, objectives, direction, and milestones.

Be externally focused. Many managers are too internally focused. You might be brilliant at managing your people and operation and executing the day-to-day deliverables you have been charged with. But are you spending enough time looking at best practices in your industry, in other sectors? Are you engaging in strategic dialogue on what others are doing? Have you created a networking circle or your own "advisory board" to counsel you on how to continue developing your people, organization, and practices? Are you reading and paying attention to future trends or disruptions that could have a significant impact on your way of doing business? Keeping a finger on the pulse of the marketplace, best practices, trends, and disruptions are critical to your long-term success.

Identify your influencers. Who are your key people within the organization who represent and reflect you and your strategy? Are they advocates for you throughout the organization and enterprise? With the executive board? In the marketplace? How are you developing these key people to be more visible and aligned with your mission, vision, and strategy to influence others? This is such an essential part of strategy that many overlook. Pay attention to having influencers that represent what you want to address. Take time to ensure they understand your message, vision, and brand.

Guard your time. As a strategic leader, you need to pay attention to where you spend your time. Are you stuck in back-to-back meetings? You can't think, plan, be externally focused, and build relationships across the enterprise if you are tied up all day in meetings or are too involved in the day-to-day. You need to shift where you spend your time by getting out of the weeds. For some of you, this will mean stopping micromanaging your people. For others, it will be about letting go of control and decision making. You can't just add hours to your day and week; take more control of your schedule versus letting your schedule dictate where you spend your time.

Each month you should take a step back and see how much time you are spending developing your bench and successors, with clients and key people throughout your enterprise, and looking at the market, competition, best practices, trends, and disruptions. Allow yourself to determine where you spend your time and ensure you are strategic about it.

Have strategic dialogue. I've worked with a number of executives who engage in a more tactical and detailed conversation when discussing their organization, initiatives, and direction. Their audience, who are anticipating a higher-level discussion, begin to tune out or disengage. Leaders need to learn how to engage in more strategic discussions. If a fellow leader is curious about the details, they will ask for a follow-up to have a more in-depth conversation, so don't take the bait to respond at the moment. Focus on the key takeaways, initiatives, and lessons learned. Highlight achievements, progress, and results. Provide context, but format it as an executive summary versus an analysis report.

Be visible. Very few leaders want to market themselves within their company and across the enterprise intentionally. It feels uncomfortable, awkward, and self-serving. Yet, you need to be visible and known by executives for potential succession and advancement. Find opportunities to meet with executives to learn about their responsibilities and the organization they run. It's an opportunity to learn about other parts of the business outside of your domain. Learn from these executives about what success looks like for them: What are their challenges? What are their vision and strategy? Educate them on these same questions for your areas of responsibility.

This is a beneficial and practical way of giving yourself a reason to be visible across the enterprise, educating others on what you are doing and accomplishing, and in learning more about the rest of the business.

Build relationships. I have gone over this in the book, but it's critical that you take the time to get to know influencers and decision-makers. People who can have an impact on your organization, capabilities, resources, results, and on your career.

Establishing trust and credibility with your team, peers, boss, and other key people in the organization gives you the capability to effectively influence, ask for input and feedback, and develop alliances, especially during critical times.

Building relationships surfaces potential advocates and mentors who will advocate for your advancement and increased scope of responsibilities, in addition to providing you guidance and advice.

Demonstrate your leadership brand. As you develop your management and leadership skills, knowledge, and capabilities, think about how you want to demonstrate your modified and developed brand to reflect who you are today. Don't assume that people are aware of your improved self. If they haven't interacted with you in a year or so, they are going by *old tapes*, their recollection, and memory of what they experienced from you previously. Demonstrate your developed brand and be consistent. This isn't to say you won't make an occasional mistake or stub your toe. Don't take for granted that people are aware of your current leadership capability and brand.

Develop your culture and talent strategy. In the following chapters, I will be going over in greater depth the need for culture and talent optimization. Leaders today need to have a strategy and plan of what kind of culture they want to have to attract and retain talent that reflects the values that are important to them in achieving their vision, mission, and purpose. What is your talent strategy that will help achieve your goals and objectives? Is your talent strategy aligned with your business strategy? How are you developing the next generation of leaders? These are all important strategic aspects of your job that you need to be developing, fine-tuning, and executing. Do you know what success looks like? Are you able to shift and modify your culture and talent strategy when needed?

Strategic leaders are agile leaders. Strategic, agile leaders are curious regarding external trends, patterns, and people. They challenge the status quo and ask disruptive questions. They are enterprise, big picture-focused, not just seeing things in their lane or sector. They weigh short- and longer-term decisions and implications. Thinking and acting strategically is the ability to use current trends and information in your decision-making and to identify and decide on the trade-offs of competing needs to move your business forward. As you plan your goals, objectives, and strategies, you need to execute and deliver results. Successful leaders can make the shift from being strategic to implementing and driving the tactics that lead to executing your deliverables. In other words, a strategic leader can *zoom in* and *zoom out*.

Why Is Being Strategic So Important?

As we've discussed, economic volatility, uncertain markets, global competitors, rapid changes in technology, and evolving workforce expectations have made leaders' jobs more unpredictable and demanding than ever. *No scenario exists today in which leaders execute in a predictable environment.*

One single formula for business success will not work, therefore being an agile leader is critical. We have seen that most of our clients abandon the five-year strategic plan and look at the world through a 24-month lens. Leaders are increasingly expected to identify new opportunities, options, and alternatives they may only vaguely understand. You evaluate a large amount of incomplete, sometimes contradictory information to identify new markets and products that don't exist today for customers who don't even know they need them yet. Being strategic and innovative is not just about having the best product anymore. Historically, you could build a successful business around a great product, but now you must ask yourself, how are you connecting with your customers and potential customers? What is the experience they will have and that you are painting? There are many inferior products, technologies, and solutions (no offense intended) that dominate their markets due to a superior go-to-market, marketing, digital, and messaging strategy. They are finding the online locations of how customers buy products and ensuring that their brand, messaging, and positioning are reaching their target audience.

While becoming a strategic leader is a tall order for many aspiring executives, and even current CEOs, it is critical given the unpredictability and complex markets we operate within—whether globally or locally. Today we must clarify what we mean about being strategic and better prepare our leaders to navigate the uncertain future.

Assess Strategy

Source: The Predictive Index

Take the doubt out of strategic alignment and execution. Whether you are on a leadership team in flux due to turnover, a new team formed through a merger or acquisition, or are trying to align your leadership team strategically, assess your leadership team utilizing the PI Strategy Assessment™.

The PI Strategy Assessment is a validated survey tool that captures a leadership team's perceptions, agreement, and confidence in their business strategy. The assessment creates a data-driven link between business strategy and talent.

How does it work?

First, leaders individually identify their top strategic priorities, then rank their confidence in the organization's ability to execute those priorities. Each statement is associated with one of four strategy types—cultivating, exploring, stabilizing, and producing—so leaders can easily visualize which strategy they're most aligned on pursuing and streamlining the actions to execute. The results' objectivity helps take the guesswork out of driving teams to strategic alignment.

What does it measure?

1. Strategy Identification – which strategies does the company need to focus on for the business to be successful?
2. Strategic Alignment – how well do people, culture, and jobs align with the demands of the strategies?
3. Organizational Readiness – is the company equipped to pursue its strategies, and what blind spots need to be addressed or monitored?

Why does it matter?

When leadership team members agree and align on strategy, they can drive toward common goals more efficiently and mitigate competing priorities to maintain focus and achieve results.

How does it help create a talent strategy?

The assessment confirms agreement on strategic priorities, identifies the strategy type and jobs to be done, and ensures the right people are in place to succeed. With strategy assessment data in hand, you have the blueprint for creating a talent strategy that bridges your business plan and results.

Chapter 19: Leadership Flux

The statistics are sobering: One out of two leaders fail within 18 months. What's worse, this statistic hasn't changed in more than 20 years. This pattern is costly in terms of turnover, engagement, succession, productivity, and financial results.

One of the primary reasons for this is that organizations don't do a good job *onboarding new leaders*. This is well-documented, but many organizations still don't take the time to improve their processes. As a result, they have to deal with the consequences of executive turnover, which are significant.

Leadership teams of all levels, types, and sizes—task forces and project teams, as well as various levels of management teams—seem to be in constant flux; therefore, *Leadership in Flux*. It's difficult getting aligned, establishing strong relationships and trust, being effective, and performing at a high level, not just for the leadership team, but for their people as well.

What are you doing to ensure that you create stability and alignment, and manage the flux to create a high-performing leadership team? What are you doing differently to onboard new leaders?

New Leader Onboarding

Leadership Landmines and How to Avoid Them. When you are onboarding into a new leadership role, landmines are everywhere. One misstep can land you in a costly trap. The harder you try to recover or rectify things, the worse they can become. Or worse, you ignore your missteps completely, assuming people will get over it. As research has shown, you have less than 90 days to establish yourself in a new leadership role, and before your key stakeholders will solidify their view of you.[23] After those 90 days, it's difficult to recover if you have crossed too many lines or stepped on too many landmines.

While some crises are unavoidable, most can be anticipated and sidestepped. A little preparation and forethought can steer you down a smoother, more impactful, and productive leadership path. Consider the following seven concepts:

Align yourself with your new boss and key stakeholders. Develop strong relationships with your key stakeholders—and influencers in the organization. Learn their roles, impact, businesses, goals, and strategies. Be crystal clear on the goals and expectations of your boss and check in regularly to ensure you are aligned. Take the time to understand the *culture* and the *operating norms* so you can learn how to modify and adjust your approach to fit in. What are *the sacred cows*? Make sure you know what have historically been untouchable policies, principles, or views.

Learn, observe, and build trust. Most new leaders want to establish themselves and their agendas and make their mark immediately. The challenge is that you know very little about the organization, culture, history, people, and where all of the landmines lie. Be patient. Listen, ask questions, learn, build relationships, and establish trust before you try to convince others of your vision and direction. Don't push people down the path; guide them as they lead the way. Don't rush into implementing your agenda! Have your people feel that you have taken the time to get to know them, their business, their history, their challenges, and their successes. Then remember, drive change *with* them, not *to* them.

---

[23] Rick Wartzman, "New employees have less than 90 days to prove themselves," Forbes, September 2015

Keep your foot out of your mouth. Listen before you speak. You can never retrieve what you have said. You may explain or clarify your comments, or even retract your statements, but the initial impact of a misspoken word will remain. A wrong assumption or casual phrase can set off a bad chain reaction. Listen to others. Ask questions. Understand the concerns and complexities before making a decision.

Don't charge into an ambush. Ask before you tell. When you have a plan in mind, ask the "what if" question. Allow staff members and stakeholders to consider it and share their support or concerns. Not only will you obtain valuable feedback and ideas for improving the plan, but you also are creating "buy-in" by enabling stakeholders to share ownership of the idea.

Serve your team, not your ego. We versus me. Share the glory, take the blame. One of the great demoralizers for staff members is the leader who takes the glory and offsets the blame. Success is a team effort. Make sure your team members are amply recognized for their work. When things don't go well, take responsibility. As a leader, you have the capability to address the problem. Take responsibility and act to rectify the issue. Throwing your staff under the bus is a recipe for failure.

Be supportive. Praise in public, correct in private. Recognize the successes of your team and publicly share their accomplishments. Encourage engagement. When correction is needed, keep the issue between you and the individual. Public humiliation causes resentment and embarrassment that demoralizes everyone.

Don't dive deep too long. You want to take a deep dive to learn the business, customers, your people, and the operation when you first begin. Once you have accomplished that, let go. Let go of the need to want to know everything. Rise to run the business, to empower and engage your people, and to operate at a strategic level.

Be aware of *the shiny new toy* **syndrome.** If you are hired from the outside or are promoted because you are the wonder kid, you represent the shiny new toy. This is similar to when a business gets excited about a potential new service, tool, product, or capability; everyone that's been involved in building the core capability of the company is disappointed and frustrated when a shiny new toy shows up. Why? Because the existing capability makes the company money, yet everyone gravitates toward the shiny new toy because it might have potential, and it might be the future. The balancing act of considering, balancing, and integrating shiny new toys with the core business is critical. It's no different for new leaders, who are also a shiny new toy; new leaders need to acknowledge the current capabilities of leaders, their people, and their accomplishments. They need to show respect, appreciation, and understanding of what used to be and where things are currently before jumping too quickly into the future.

Agile leadership involves stepping forward into the unknown and making decisions for a team. It can be risky, but with just a few simple concepts in mind, you can minimize your chances of detonating some of the most common leadership traps when onboarding.

I was once asked to work with an executive that had been with a very large and successful company as a member of the C-team, who was hired to transform a significant part of the business. The problem was that he had destroyed trust and collaboration with his leadership team. By the time I met with him, his reputation was beyond repair. A brief example: he began the first meeting with his new team by informing them of all the issues that needed to be resolved, and of how he was going to transform the organization. The problem was, he was dictating to them, not involving them. Even worse, he hadn't been there long enough to establish relationships, trust, and credibility. He didn't understand the culture or the history of the organization and why they were where they were. Instead, he unintentionally threw them all under the bus. He informed them that, in a way, they were responsible for why the organization was where it was!

Avoid these common landmines and focus on what is needed to onboard within your first 90 days, so you don't become one of two leaders who do not make it in 18 months.

Reboot

Even in this age of flux, some leadership teams have been together for a long time. The average tenure of a CEO is about three years, so five years or more can be considered unusually long. This stability is valuable, but the challenge is teams that have been together for a number of years can become stale. They are used to each other and take each other for granted. As a result, they don't challenge each other, and they lose effectiveness. They have grown too comfortable.

Sometimes, a reboot is needed. If you are leading a legacy team, take it upon yourself to reinvigorate the team by challenging the status quo and creating the spark of a new lens, a new approach—in how you make decisions, communicate, and work with each other, from an individual and team standpoint. Add a new member to the team to reinvigorate innovation and provide an outside perspective. Provide new assignments for current leaders to gain fresh perspectives. You need to look at things differently, get out of your routine and comfort zone, make sure you are relevant to and understanding of the marketplace, and have not lost critical external value.

Have you been together for a long time and need a reboot? Though we may fear and resist change, it is necessary. How are you managing the flux? What can you do to take your leadership impact to the next level?

Habits of Effective Senior Leadership Teams

Great businesses align their people strategy with their business strategy for optimal results. But if your senior leaders aren't *also* aligned with the company's core values (i.e., the behaviors your organization needs to succeed), your employees won't be either.

Senior leadership team dynamics are essential to leadership alignment, team, and organizational culture.

Senior leadership teams deal with behavioral similarities and differences and work together to achieve a common goal, just like any other team.

The big difference is that all eyes are on the senior leaders, and behaviors trickle down from the top. Employees look to executives to set the tone when it comes to culture, rewarded behaviors, and teamwork. *You can't outsource setting a good example.*

What are you trying to accomplish as an executive team? Those objectives should lend themselves to behaviors required for success (e.g., if your leadership team needs to spearhead change, you'll need to innovate and take risks). Assess your current leadership team to determine alignment between each individual and your desired behavioral traits.

Consider how your current team dynamic might support or hinder efforts to achieve your objectives. If, for example, some of your leaders are wired to innovate while others are wired to create processes, you would likely end up with competing goals. These competing goals could create conflict, inhibiting results. By aligning on objectives and behaviors required for success, senior leaders can put aside personal preferences to focus on supporting the business strategy. For some, this might mean stretching outside their natural behavioral tendencies (e.g., a process-oriented executive might move at a faster-than-normal pace to support the organization's goal of rapid growth).

Your senior leadership team needs to present a united front. Conflict amongst team members can ripple out and impact the entire organization.

A leading cause of interpersonal conflict is behavioral differences. Senior leaders can create awareness around behavioral similarities and differences by leveraging people data/talent analytic tools such as PI, as discussed in previous chapters.

With this people data in hand, senior leaders can pinpoint potential problem areas between team members and proactively work to address them. For example, if most of the team is highly extraverted, but one member of the team has low extraversion, that team member could stretch to make sure they're heard during meetings—or the rest of the team could actively create opportunities for that person's voice to be heard. ("Liz, what are your thoughts on this subject?")

The goal isn't to build a leadership team that's wired to behave the same across the board—that can lead to groupthink, less creativity, and exaggerated weaknesses. Behavioral differences provide balance—the key is to negotiate differences so everyone can do their job well. For example, an executive who's wired to protect the company from risk might need to become more willing to take a *calculated* risk. An executive who's wired to take risks and move quickly might need to slow down a little to take more *thoughtful* risks.

Leadership Team Awareness and Capability

I have been fortunate to work with many outstanding and successful executive teams. The challenge of leadership teams that are in flux is not going away. Leaders need to pay close attention to their team's effectiveness. It begins with self-awareness. Leaders need to know each other's motivations and drives, as well as their behavioral profiles and strengths. This openness and transparency, which I've seen many executive teams struggle with, will provide insight into why some executives are so assertive, and some are not. Referencing behavioral profiles will reveal why some executives are so connecting and opinionated, while others are more observant and reserved. You may have noticed that some leaders want to move quickly and decisively, and some want to slow things down and continue to evaluate and look at data; some want to debate and butt heads, but others want to stay in their lane and may shut down if they feel attacked; some will be risk-averse, and some will want to take more risks. You will observe that some leaders want to operate in the details, process, and tactics, while others want to focus on the big picture.

What are the behavioral analytics of your leadership team? Do they understand each other, especially when they are coming and going as team members? Do they each understand the implications and impact of these differences and similarities? Do they know how to effectively navigate the differences so they can become a highly functional and performing team? I often use PI's team analytics to understand a team's leadership style. This helps reveal the gaps in becoming a high-performing leadership team.

Do you know if the profile of your leadership team is in line with what your business strategy is? For example, if you are looking to drive innovation and growth, head into new and uncharted waters, and take certain calculated risks, does your leadership team's style and personality reflect these attributes and characteristics? If you are looking to stabilize your organization after a significant merger or restructure, engage your employees, or have a greater focus on recognition and reward, does your leadership team possess these capabilities? Using PI, you can learn and understand the makeup of your team, its strengths and gaps, and what development and changes you need to make to align your leadership team with your strategic objectives.

The following are sample leadership team analytics showing how you can assess the alignment and strengths of your team per the leadership and strategic initiatives, needs, and direction of your business:

Overall Team Work Styles

Teamwork and Employees Experience:
- Developing and empowering employees
- Fostering collaboration
- Increasing loyalty and commitment

Process and Precision:
- Increasing efficiency
- Increasing reliability
- Implementing control and structure

Innovation and Agility:
- Leading innovation and vision
- Growing rapidly
- Implementing change
- Increasing agility

Results and Discipline:
- Focus on customer
- Delivering results
- Maximizing profitability

Communication Styles

Connecting:
- Sensitive to people and feelings
- Relationship building
- External focus

Respecting:
- Pleasant, professional
- Strong view, respect others
- Internal focus

Persuading:
- Influencing others
- Build networks, gain support
- External focus

Telling:
- Loud, assertive
- Fast-moving
- Internal focus

Taking Action Styles

Implementing:
- Methodical, structured
- Detain-oriented

Commanding:
- Strong opinion on "right" way

Coordinating:
- Genuine relationships
- Alignment

Innovating:
- Challenge status-quo
- New ways

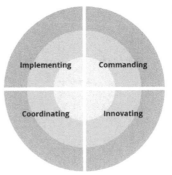

Source: The Predictive Index

Drive Culture

Culture has to start from the top down. It's not something executives are exempt from or should relegate to HR. The senior leadership team has to be intentional in modeling the company culture.

How the executive team works together will inform how other teams work together. For example, if the CEO's ideas reign supreme on the executive team—as compared to where all executives' opinions are vetted equally—this behavior will trickle down to other team levels. If your organization requires an increase in collaboration, your leadership team should be modeling this behavior. We will talk more about company culture in chapter 20.

Growth Mindset

The modern work environment gets disrupted very quickly with new competitors, new technology, and changing market conditions. This increased volatility demands more flexibility from organizations. The key to flexibility is a *growth mindset*, which is the belief that basic abilities can be developed through dedication and hard work. This is the opposite of a fixed mindset or a belief that you're born with and limited to a certain amount of talent or ability.

High growth is a goal that all senior leadership teams can agree upon. For top business leaders, a growth mindset means *being willing to learn and grow*. Learning shouldn't stop because you've reached the C-suite. It's critical you continue to learn and grow to be most effective in your role and to model that behavior for others. High growth mindset leaders establish an environment of openness, transparency, and risk-taking; they embrace failure and encourage teams to accept failure. They create a culture of development, challenging themselves and their people to develop new skills and abilities and new ways of thinking. High growth mindset leaders promote from within as often as possible but also integrate new hires to bring new perspectives, experiences, and disruption.

Create Alignment

How can you make sure that you and your team stay in alignment with your strategy, vision, mission, purpose, goals, and with each other? With so many moving parts, changes, and shifts, and with the intense speed of change, it can be easy for people to go off and head in many different directions. Soon it feels like no one is on the same page.

I suggest having a quarterly one-on-one meeting with everyone who reports directly to you. In each of these meetings, address six key questions. Ideally, each question will result in a two-way dialogue that helps clarify priorities, ensure alignment, and promote mutual understanding:

Where are we going? As the manager, share your views on critical priorities for the larger organization. Then ask for your subordinate's views. This dialogue will help ensure alignment between your and their perspective when it comes to what matters.

Where are you going? Ask what direction they are heading. Then give your view on where this person and their part of the business should be going. This dialogue will help ensure alignment between your management of the larger organization and their management of their part of your organization.

What are you doing well? Ask them to share their perception of what they are doing well. Then share your view on their key achievements. Sometimes our lack of recognition is not a function of apathy; it is a function of not understanding accomplishments from the other person's perspective. By asking this, we can see where they're coming from and what they value.

What changes can lead to improvement? Ask for ideas on how more progress can be made in the future. Then, share your thoughts. Be open to the possibility that their ideas may be better than yours.

How can I help? Ask for feedback on how you can better help them achieve agreed upon goals. If you want to be a great developer of future leaders, this question is fundamental.

What suggestions do you have for me? Ask for their ideas on changes you can make to become a more effective manager. If you want them to focus on continuous improvement, you can lead by example. Demonstrate the importance of asking for feedback from others.

Leadership teams need to establish *shared responsibility* and *shared ownership* for continued alignment and effectiveness. Your team needs to reach out if they are ever uncertain about priorities or need feedback. As the leader, you need to set the tone by approaching your team if the business changes or shifts, or if you need to reset priorities. Hopefully, they will then mirror this approach with their direct reports, and so on.

Chapter 20: Develop High Performing Teams

Developing Effective Teams

Great teams are the building blocks of any organization. A great team has shared goals, clear roles, transparent processes for solving problems and making decisions, and the ability to deal with conflicts constructively. A good team may have some of these elements, but a great team will have them all. It's up to you as a leader to make sure all of these elements are in place.

There are three key dimensions of great teamwork. The first is alignment on direction: There should be a shared belief about what the company is striving toward and the team's role in getting there. The second is high-quality interaction: The team should be characterized by trust, open communication, and a willingness to embrace conflict. The third is a strong sense of renewal: There should be an environment in which team members are energized by feeling they can take risks, innovate, learn from outside ideas, and achieve something that matters—often against the odds.

Want to build your own high-performing team? Here are the qualities shared by teams that go above and beyond to achieve results.

It's About Respect. Respect is a crucial requirement for a healthy team and work environment. It promotes increased productivity, efficiency, and growth. It lets team members know they are valued for their abilities, qualities, and achievements, and that their role is vital to the team and organization's success.

Being respected and valued promotes a positive culture in which employees are loyal, fulfilled, and motivated to perform at their best. Those who are not respectful of others are unprofessional and a threat to the health of their company.

Treat people the way you want to be treated—with respect. Recognize that, like you, your colleagues have rights, opinions, wishes, experience, and competence. They also make mistakes, which are simply lessons to be learned. They have similar concerns and insecurities and share the common goal of wanting to perform their jobs successfully.

Respect opinions, experiences, backgrounds, and differences. We may not always agree or like a member of our team, but we need to respect them. It may mean agreeing to disagree. If we want to receive respect, we need to demonstrate it.

It's About Trust. Trust is crucial for a high-performing team to succeed. A team without trust can't be inspired, resolve conflicts, embrace stretch goals, or communicate effectively. The lack of trust slows down everything.

Set Clear Expectations and Responsibilities. High-performing teams need to have clear and defined roles, responsibilities, and specifics on what success looks like. As that changes—and it most likely will—teams need to continue to communicate and provide input and feedback when and where it's needed.

Lack of trust is what turns team members against each other. And when there is no trust, there's no room for safety, innovation, or risk-taking. I've found that there are five pillars that build trust.

Relationships. We tend to reserve our trust for people that we know. We trust our friends and distrust our enemies. Building a positive relationship between team members increases trust.

Knowledge. We trust people who provide the right answer when we need it or people who can provide insight into a situation or problem. We tend to trust people the most when they can help solve problems. Use your knowledge and skills to help others solve a problem, and it will increase trust. Allow members of your high-performing team to shine and show their knowledge and expertise to further cement that trust.

Consistency. When you say you will do something and follow through, people will trust you. Being consistent with all team members will foster greater trust because they know that you mean what you say.

Accountability. As a leader, your role is to hold each team member accountable for pulling their weight and meeting their performance objectives. If you don't, the rest of the team will disengage and check out and not fulfill their objectives. It also means holding yourself accountable.

Empowerment. To reach stretch goals, high-performing teams must be empowered to be critical thinkers, innovative, and comfortable with making mistakes, and making decisions. I've mentioned already that leaders need to "let go"—empowering your team is part of that.

Inspire Instead of Push. High-performance teams are skilled at creating energy and enthusiasm. Team members feel inspired when they know they are on a mission. They feel that what they are doing is of great importance.

Resolve Differences and Work Together. High-performing teams know that conflicts can tear teams apart. They understand the need to resolve differences quickly and promote cooperation. Low-performing teams assume that mature people will step in to resolve conflict.

High-performing teams address problems quickly and directly before they get worse. When you create an environment in which people believe that others have their back, disputes are easier to resolve. It's also okay to agree to disagree sometimes; you are trying to create *one voice* as a team, which requires openness, transparency, and addressing all issues. That requires compromise and alignment. Teams that focus on cooperation versus competition achieve outstanding results.

Constant Communication. It's easy for anyone to get distracted or miss a turn. To keep a high-performing team focused on the vision, it's okay to sound like a "broken record," especially at first. High-performance teams must stay on message so they will constantly communicate and keep other people focused on the vision and mission they're trying to accomplish. Sometimes team members can get distracted from their mission. Leaders of high-performance teams keep their people informed and up to date so they can stay on track.

Set "Stretch" Goals. Create stretch goals for your team and generate an internal drive to accomplish the impossible. People aren't apt to do extraordinary things without motivation. When you set stretch goals, you help your team recognize what they are personally capable of. Inspiring your team to achieve something out of the ordinary helps them see how exceptional they can be when they work together. Do this and watch their engagement and pride skyrocket.

Key Traits of Successful Agile Teams

Agile teams are small, entrepreneurial groups designed to stay close to customers and adapt quickly to changing conditions. When implemented correctly, this results in higher team productivity and morale, faster time to market, better quality, and lower risk than traditional approaches can achieve. They are small and multidisciplinary. Given a significant, complex problem, they develop solutions through rapid problem solving and idea and solution development with tight feedback loops. They place more value on adapting to change than on sticking to a plan.

Let's begin by looking at key characteristics of successful agile teams:

Comfort with change. Agile teams are flexible and able to operate in a continually changing environment.

Comfort with uncertainty. Agile teams are designed to thrive in ambiguous situations full of intriguing questions but few clear answers.

Collaboration. Being agile is a team sport, and agile teams know how to blend different perspectives, expertise, and skills for maximum effectiveness.

Decisiveness. Agile teams make imperfect decisions every day, but what's most important is that they make decisions; they don't endlessly debate and contemplate.

Discipline. Agile teams take a disciplined approach to executing a well-designed process. They develop processes, checks, and balances, achieve milestones, and focus on the plan and projected deliverables.

Initiative. Agile teams have a bias for action; inaction is a recipe for missed opportunities if not outright disaster.

Speed. Agile teams realize the need to capitalize on opportunities and to reduce learning cycles.

Like any business challenge, the risks associated with building agile teams are people challenges. Certain types of people are naturally wired to some of these agile characteristics but may struggle with others.

Some people easily demonstrate initiative and are comfortable with change, but they may need to "stretch" to accommodate the required rigor of discipline. By contrast, other people are naturally adept at the process and discipline required for agile performance but may struggle to operate in an environment of ambiguity without proper coaching and support.

How to Build Agile Teams

Teams must be fit for the task at hand. A major business trend is the rise of the agile team and organization. Companies of all sizes and in virtually all industries are creating agile teams to get closer to customers and adapt to rapidly changing business environments. *Agile teams are innovative, collaborative, and nimble.* They outperform bureaucratic and hierarchical team structures for many types of work in the modern world.

As an *Agile Leader*, you'll likely be asked to build and lead agile teams and organizations. To do so, you'll need to understand the characteristics of high-performing agile teams and the steps required to get your team ready to take the field.

Let's look at some specific actions you should and should not take when building agile teams:

Keep team sizes small. Large teams can't be as nimble as they need to be. Communication, action, and decision-making flow more freely in smaller teams operating in an agile mode.

Be aligned on purpose, strategy, and goals. When constructing a team, lead a thoughtful review of the team's objectives, scope, and required cross-functional skills.

Raise awareness. Use behavioral data like with PI to understand and review each team member's natural strengths and challenges related to working in an agile mode.

Don't pigeonhole people. While individuals may not be naturally wired to adopt certain agile practices, always keep a growth mindset. People can flex their behaviors, given sufficient motivation, coaching, and feedback.

Don't set people up to fail. There are limits to how much stretch is possible—and therefore is fair to ask of people. Rather than assign agile work to someone most comfortable in roles requiring predictability and freedom from making mistakes, it's better to find more traditional work assignments for this contributor.

To succeed in an agile business environment, build your teams in a purposeful way. This will inevitably demand a thoughtful and tailored leadership approach from you and a willingness to flex and accommodate some unnatural behaviors from your team members.

If you're committed to getting this right, you'll tap into any and all available people data, using tools like PI to maximize awareness and guide your coaching over time as you build your team's agile capabilities.

Your people make your organization unique; they set you apart from every other company and drive your company's success. By developing strong teams, you enable your people to solve problems better and accomplish shared goals. Creating strong, agile teams is one of the most important things you can do as a leader.

Chapter 21: Create Culture

A Framework for Culture

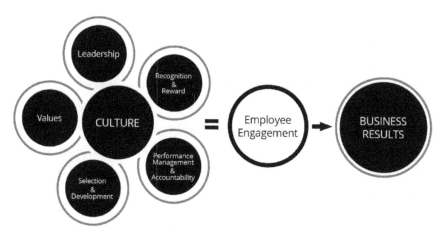

Source: Chuck Mollor, MCG Partners

I designed this cultural model to illustrate the driving forces that create a strong and aligned culture to achieve a highly engaged, productive workforce that delivers business results. Let's go over some of it in this chapter.

Leaders Create Culture

We've gone over many aspects of what is essential for a leader to be successful today and in the future, including creating alignment, communicating a vision and purpose, and building the next generation of leaders. But leaders must also create a *culture*.

How do you create a culture that reflects the vision, purpose, and values of your organization? A culture that not only attracts a certain kind of person but also develops and retains that talent?

In the latest Vistage CEO Confidence Index survey, which captured insights from 1,518 CEOs and business leaders, only one in six respondents said they were satisfied with the strength of their organizational culture![24]

The more connected an employee feels to the organization's culture, the more likely they will be to go above their job description and work harder, longer, and more creatively. Creating a positive culture that invests in people and develops leaders is an essential part of being an agile leader.

Companies like Apple, Google, and LinkedIn have unique cultures. Many biotech and tech companies are known for their relaxed atmospheres, unique team structures, and employee benefits. For the most part, these companies are also known for providing excellent products or services to their customers or groundbreaking research. An emphasis on people, quality, learning, and leadership development, and a focus on values are all important components of a thriving culture.

Some organizations are known for having a negative or undesirable culture. People who go to work for these companies are aware that often they are entering an environment where it is necessary to step on others to climb to the top, or where people don't walk the talk regarding values, amongst a number of other attributes. Some people thrive in those environments, and some of those companies deliver excellent products.

Changing an organization's culture requires a change in leadership or a shift in leadership's mindset. Culture does not grow from the grassroots. While the workforce and customers can grow weary and demand a change, the impetus must still come from the top.

Microsoft was known as a hard-edged, performance-driven, competitive culture for many years. In 2014, a new CEO came on board. Soft spoken and people-oriented, he was very different from

24 Anne Petrik, "5 Tips for Reinforcing Culture," Vistage, 2019

the previous CEO. He brought his own philosophy and style and made changes to how the company made decisions. In less than a decade, the entire culture changed, and Microsoft's value dramatically increased. According to one engineer, "What changed was leadership, and everything followed from that."

Nothing can change, create, and drive the culture of an organization like deliberate, agile leadership.

The Impact of an Unhealthy Culture

We've all had days where the productive person who walked through the door in the morning lost steam by mid-afternoon. There are a variety of factors that can kill work productivity, including poor job fit and being forced to work alongside low performers. An unhealthy culture fit tops the list.

Recently, 1,000 people were asked one question: *What are your biggest productivity killers?* Tasked with choosing between boss, culture, job fit, or team, the majority said culture problems are the biggest factor affecting work productivity.

What makes an organization unique is its culture. A strong, intentional, and well-communicated organizational culture is the foundation of any good company and what sets it apart from its competitors. Strong organizational culture is what helps companies win accolades like Glassdoor's *Best Places to Work* award, and it's integral to employee retention. Culture is what attracts candidates to apply to a company job posting and entices them to sign on the dotted line once an offer is made.

Lack of fit hurts culture and employee productivity. But what happens when an organization's culture is the very reason for employee disengagement? One of the four forces that disrupt employee engagement and productivity is a lack of fit with company culture. There are a number of things that can create and breed toxicity in an organization. For example, it's crucial to always let employees know where they stand. If you are not actively speaking with and discussing where your people stand, be aware of the disengagement and the resulting drop in productivity that undoubtedly will follow.

Employees want to "fit" with their organization's culture. They want to feel as if they're part of something positive, a culture of values they are in line with, and a mission they can get behind and support.

While screening candidates for culture fit is something that should always happen during the hiring process, the reality is that it rarely happens. Companies end up with a workforce of people who don't align with their organizational values and culture. This is detrimental to the company's bottom line. Employees who are misaligned with their company culture will never go the extra mile or put in "extra" discretionary effort. When employees are aligned with their company culture, they work extra hard to help the company reach its strategic goals and outperform their less-engaged colleagues.

How a toxic organization can destroy culture. While culture is designed in the C-suite, it's lived and perpetuated by the employees of all levels. Organizations enter dangerous waters when the message on their "about us" page contradicts the message their employees display day in and day out. Many factors create a toxic workplace. If any of the following factors ring true for you, you'll want to take corrective action as soon as possible:

- You don't have your core values outlined and articulated.
- Your employees don't know your company values.

- Your processes and procedures don't align with your core values.
- Your managers and employees do not demonstrate the values that reflect the culture you want.
- There is no accountability if managers and employees do not demonstrate those values.
- You don't pay attention to the *behavioral drives and needs* of yourselves and each other.
- You place people in roles that they're not naturally wired to do.
- Your managers don't provide regular feedback.
- There is not strong enough or consistent accountability or feedback for non-performance.
- Your managers and employees are entitled.
- Your people are resistant to changes happening in the organization.

So, how can you help your people get on board with your organizational culture to minimize toxicity and maximize engagement and work productivity?

You don't want your employees' minds consumed with thoughts like whether they're aligning with your culture. It should be more organic than that, and it should come from the top-down.

Agile leaders know that they must create a value proposition for why people would want to work for their company, stay there, and develop a career. That's all wrapped around culture. What do we value, recognize, and reward? How do we inspire, develop, and promote? Your views on that will become part of the culture you help create.

Maximize work productivity by following these best practices for designing, communicating, and enforcing organizational culture. Here are tips for designing an award-winning culture, clearly communicating that culture to everyone in the organization, and ensuring all employees are aligned with it.

Be sure your organizational culture aligns with your business strategy. Your culture must align with your company's strategic goals. If your strategy is to innovate, you can't have a culture where work is expected to be 100% error-free, or else. Innovation involves risk-taking, and risk-taking involves failure. Your culture should celebrate risk-taking (reasonable, calculated) and accept that failure is part of the journey.

You need employees who are crystal clear on what your strategic goals are so they can work toward executing them. When your culture reflects your strategy, you set your employees up for success. Let's say you're focused on new product development; you'll want to design a culture of innovation where failure is framed as a learning experience rather than something negative.

Some smart companies ask their employees to participate in the creation of their culture and the values that reflect the culture. If you're interested in doing this, get employees across all departments together for various brainstorming sessions, order some food, and talk it out as a group. Ask yourselves: What behaviors, attributes and characteristics are required to execute our business strategy? What do we stand for? What do we value? How do we make decisions?

These brainstorming sessions ensure that your people understand your culture and feel like they were a part of creating it. It also brings to the surface any lingering questions and acts as an outlet for employees to air any concerns regarding current culture.

Identify gaps between culture and strategy and work to close them. Use tools like *engagement surveys* and *focus groups* to measure how well your employees currently understand and align with your company culture. Chances are you're going to find some gaps, especially if your employees weren't involved in its creation.

There are various ways to close those gaps. You can update your rewards and recognition systems; do this by promoting employees who embody your values, and then communicating the reason why they were promoted, so everyone understands. Another method is to develop a shared language in which you weave cultural values into everyday conversation; for example, if a core value is "energy," talk about it at every team and all-company meeting, and also encourage employees to give public shout-outs to peers who embody this cultural value on a dedicated *Slack channel* or appropriate venue.

Update your performance management system and process. Managers and employees should be assessed on their effectiveness at demonstrating the values and behaviors that reflect your culture, in addition to their ability to achieve goals and perform. If this isn't the case, the values and mission that are framed all over your offices, break rooms, front lobby, and conference rooms, and listed on your website, mean nothing.

It's no secret that highly productive employees give companies a competitive advantage. The more effort you take to design, communicate, and nurture a strong organizational culture, the more rewards you'll reap.

Tips for Changing Culture Within an Organization

As a leader, it's your responsibility to identify the source of disengagement and act on it.

We've identified *four main forces of employee disengagement*. One alone can cripple your organization. Two or more can be fatal. All four involve misalignment between the employee and one of the following: **role, manager, team, and culture.**

Misalignment with Role

Forty-six percent of new hires fail within 18 months. For many, that failure is predestined by a faulty hiring system. Eighty-two percent of hiring managers surveyed acknowledge they prioritized resumes and skill checkboxes over more reliable predictors of a good match—coachability, emotional intelligence, motivation, and temperament. Research shows that job fit is a key indicator of employee engagement; it's crucial to get it right from the start.

Misalignment with Manager

In the U.S., 75% of employees cite their manager as the worst part of their job. A whopping 65% would take a pay cut in exchange for changing bosses. Where's the disconnect? Only 21% of employees believe their managers have what it takes to motivate them to do outstanding work. They don't trust their bosses, so they check out. This is why ensuring manager fit by giving managers the training and tools they need to inspire effectively is critical.

Misalignment with Team

"Go, Team!" It should be a rallying cry for a group effort, but in offices where disengagement is rampant, it can sound more like nails scraping a chalkboard. Add cross-functional reporting and a geographically diverse workforce, and the potential for cohesive and productive teamwork takes a nosedive. Eighty-six percent of workers surveyed cite a lack of collaboration and ineffective communication as the root causes of team failure.

Misalignment with Culture

In his 1943 paper "A Theory of Human Motivation," 20th-century psychologist Abraham Maslow introduced a hierarchy of needs. More than 75 years later, Maslow's hierarchy—physiological, safety, love and belonging, esteem, and self-actualization—still rings true. Noticeably, love, and belonging rank as more basic human needs than esteem and self-actualization. It's no small wonder, then, that lack of corporate culture, the foundation of belonging, is among the top causes of employee disengagement.

So how can you identify which of these four forces is causing your engagement and productivity problems?

You can diagnose the problem by collecting and measuring your people data. If you suspect that the problem might be culture, survey your employees. Examine the magnitude of the problem to determine how fast you need to act.

A cultural disconnect affects your bottom line. Citing studies by the Queens School of Business and Gallup, Harvard Business Review revealed some startling statistics on the cost of disengagement. Disengaged workers had:

- 37% higher absenteeism
- 49% more accidents
- 60% more errors and defects[25]

Moreover, organizations with low employee engagement scores experience:

---

[25] Michelle Boeldt, "How Engaged Workers Are Safe Employees," EHS Today, August 2017

- 18% lower productivity
- 16% lower profitability
- 37% lower job growth

The Engagement Institute estimates $450–550 billion in losses stemming from employee disengagement.[26]

The fix?

Changing culture within an organization can boost employee engagement and productivity.

A strong, intentional, and well-communicated organizational culture is the foundation for setting a company apart from its competitors. In a study of 100 organizations, Northwestern University researchers found that companies with satisfied employees also had a higher percentage of satisfied customers.[27] These customers purchased the company's products more frequently, maintained higher levels of loyalty, and reported greater satisfaction, which directly contributed to higher gross margins, higher repeat business, and reduced acquisition costs for each company.

But how do you shape or fix your company's culture? Get started with these tips.

Be open to your desired culture. Be transparent about the type of culture you are trying to create. Hold an all-company meeting and talk through what your ideal culture looks like and any steps you plan to take to get there. Then repeat, including updates on progress, often.

---

[26] Valerie Bolden-Barrett, "Study: Disengaged Employees Can Cost Companies Up To $550B a Year," HR Dive, March 2017
[27] Terrie Nolinske, Ph.D., "The Value of Surveying Employees and Customers," National Business Research Institute

Anticipate friction and resistance. Speaking of taking steps to get there, know that any changes you make will ruffle some employees' feathers. Some people with high patience are naturally wired to be resistant to change. Expect resistance and be prepared to explain the "why" behind what you're doing.

Make sure candidates are a cultural fit. We talk a lot about hiring smart by making workplace assessments like PI part of the process. But it's also critical to ensure candidate cultural fit as part of the hiring process. Have every member of the interview team ask questions designed to probe into whether a candidate fits with your organizational culture and have them use a rubric to score.

Reward employees who embody the culture you're trying to build. Want employees to adopt your culture? Publicly reward employees who embody your cultural values. In our example above of the innovative company, you might want to promote someone at that company who consistently innovates and improves the product line, so everyone sees that type of behavior is rewarded.

It's also important to note that culture isn't a one-time thing. You should regularly measure and monitor your culture to ensure it continues to align with your strategy and inspire your people to go the extra mile to help your company succeed.

A High Performing Culture

A high-performance culture is one that focuses on the employee experience and the customer experience to drive better business results. Every organization has goals it is trying to achieve. The culture leaders at these organizations create should be focused on driving performance toward those goals. A high-performing culture has certain aspects which include:

A change mindset. It all starts with a shift in mindset. To successfully lead, you need to embrace a mindset that allows you to recognize when change is needed, and to be always asking yourself "what do I need to be doing differently to be a high-performing business or organization?" You need to think beyond your current capabilities and be pushed outside of your comfort zone. You should be thinking about continuous improvement: what needs to be addressed, do I have the right resources, who's overloaded? Do I have the strategy, structure, and processes?

Empowered people making decisions. To foster a high-performing culture, you need to get out of your own way and give permission for managers and employees to empower themselves. High-performing cultures have highly motivated employees who have decision-making capabilities. The key is how to let go, not being involved in everything, not knowing everything, and trusting them to solve problems. If you can't, then you have the wrong people.

Culture of accountability. You need to surround yourself with people who want accountability and will own it. High-performing cultures have people who have input into and ownership of their roles and goals, so that when conditions change—which they will— they have the freedom and ability to pivot and modify the objectives and related tasks. When people own accountability, they address those who are not carrying their weight and are not accountable.

Identified values. Values make your company a better place to work and more profitable. Your values need to drive everyone's behaviors each day. Trustworthiness and fairness need to be demonstrated each day.

Formed community. Unity and community create conditions for strong employee cooperation and culture. This fosters winning together when times are good and sticking together when times are tough.

Reinforced positive behavior. Develop a positive can-do attitude. Recognize and reward individuals and teams who represent the values of the organization to increase the likelihood of repetition and of others following.

Transparent communication. Ensure the flow of information is smooth, from and to every employee and in every direction. Communication, information, education, updates, challenges, failures, and obstacles — they all need to be shared, discussed, and clarified.

Constant feedback. A feedback-rich culture is key for a high-performing culture. Employees who feel comfortable providing feedback are more apt to challenge the status quo on anything. Not having any *sacred cows* — items that are untouchable — allows you to have an open environment where everyone is comfortable with providing input and feedback, so you don't end up finding comments on Glassdoor and other social media sites with negative opinions. Transparent feedback will help you find out how employees are feeling about culture, systems, processes, decisions, and strategies, and whether anything needs to be improved. Take the feedback anytime and anywhere, take them seriously, and take action!

Connecting the Dots

I had a client that wanted a strong culture that reflected the organization's brand, strategy, and values, but it wasn't working. We did an employee engagement survey, and the results were good, but not great. A primary issue that came out of the survey was the lack of trust in and accountability of leadership. I asked what they were doing in their performance management process to assess and provide feedback to all managers and employees regarding how they demonstrated company values. It turns out, they were not doing anything. In other words, they had these wonderful values that reflected the brand and culture they aspired to be, but a manager or employee could not demonstrate their values, and they wouldn't be evaluated or held accountable.

A mistake many organizations' leadership teams make when creating values that reflect the culture they aspire to have, is *they don't connect the dots.*

As my cultural model image at the beginning of this chapter demonstrates, you must integrate and align the dots connecting: your performance management process and system; with rewards and compensation; promotions and succession; selection and hiring; and behaviors that all employees need to demonstrate to reflect the cultural values you expect each day.

If you want a strong culture to reflect your internal and external brand and achieve your strategic and business objectives, connect the dots.

Invest in Your People

Research shows that bad leaders lose money, while the best leaders often more than double the profits of leaders who are good or average. Many factors contribute to gains and losses, but the facts show that effective leadership drives profit. Companies like Starbucks have indicated that *employee commitment and happiness leads to an increase in customer satisfaction, and happy customers spend more money.*

Some factors that are known to increase profitability include employee satisfaction, low turnover, and high levels of commitment. Most of these factors are directly influenced by the quality of leadership.

Investing in your employees should include training to help them learn their roles and responsibilities, along with the technical aspects of their jobs. Training your new supervisors and managers on how to manage their people on a daily basis is critical. Develop managers at all levels, including the C-suite. I see many organizations stop development when people reach the C-suite. However, the C-suite needs to continue their improvement as leaders, and it sends the wrong message if they feel they are above improvements, and everyone else continues working toward improvement. I also see many organizations focus development resources and efforts to only senior leadership, but don't have much in place for new and mid-level managers. This is a problem as mid-level managers are managing the majority of employees and need those critical managerial skills. Other non-traditional education includes job rotations, task forces, committees, and projects. Providing mentorship and mentee opportunities, including reverse mentorships, engages all levels of employees in their development. *Your employees are looking for opportunities to learn to grow!*

Extraordinary leaders exhibit certain qualities, including being results-oriented and good with people, having outstanding character, and being able to lead through change. Most people are not born with these qualities—but they can all be learned. Take the time to learn to be an excellent Agile Leader. Commit to developing these qualities in your leaders. Care about your people, their lives, and their families. Be passionate about managing them, coaching them, developing them, and helping them achieve their dreams and ambitions.

If you are going to invest enough to employ people in your organization, it makes sense to invest in their development and engagement. And if you want them to be productive and stay, continue to invest in your development as a leader as well.

Chapter 22: Managing Change

"It is not the strongest of the species that survives, nor the most intelligent that survives. It is the one that is most adaptable to change." – Charles Darwin

Change Is the New Normal

Change is no longer an event; it's constant. Many leaders are realizing that to effectively deal with today's change and the next inevitable one, *they need to be more agile about change.* In order to do so, deliberate actions must be taken to embed change in the organization in order to have a sustainable and effective impact.

Change management is outdated. Research shows that 70% of change programs fail to achieve their goals, largely due to employee resistance and lack of management support.[28] This translates to an ineffective change management strategy and implementation.

However, companies with good change management practices are 3.5 times more likely to outperform their peer organizations. Companies with a change management approach have 2.5 times greater financial returns[29].

Whatever the reason for a change initiative in an organization, my experience with clients is that these types of transitions typically bring a unique set of challenges that, if not managed properly, can lead to failure. How can you make sure your organization doesn't end up on the wrong side of that statistic?

---

[28] Boris Ewenstein, Wesley Smith, and Ashvin Sologar, "Changing Change Management," McKinsey, July 2015

[29] Connie Folk, "The Inconvenient Truths About Organizational Change Management," Column 5 Consulting, June 2015

Consider the most common reasons why change initiatives fail:

- Miscommunication of expectations
- Leadership misalignment
- Cultural misalignment
- Organizational misalignment
- Lack of clarity of the "new world order"
- Inexperienced managers
- Insufficient change in leadership skills
- Inadequate internal commitment
- Shortfall of executive sponsorship
- Barriers, including processes or structures, that are not removed or addressed
- Deficient reinforcement regarding new behaviors and systems reflecting the "new" culture

What's the common denominator underscoring these causes? You guessed it: People!

Change can evoke fear in some people—a fear of what is being lost versus what will be gained. While that fear can result in people hindering your change efforts (unintentionally or otherwise), given the proper tools, support, and environment, these folks can be empowered to help themselves and others spearhead change initiatives.

Organizations that experience success during times of change typically create a framework that is supported by these components:

- Establishing trust, openness, and relationships with key change sponsors and owners
- Communicating the need for change *often* to different audiences utilizing multiple channels

- If a merger or acquisition, identifying the characteristics of your team, the other leadership team, and both organizations' cultures
- Homing in on critical behaviors and skills that accelerate performance
- Assessing strengths, weaknesses, motivating needs, and drives to optimize talent
- Nurturing an atmosphere of open collaboration and a safe work environment
- Getting executive sponsors to establish a vision and set a clear direction
- Evaluating the change process and adjusting the strategy as needed

While it's not uncommon for conflicts to arise from misalignment and misunderstanding during times of change, taking the time to understand the motivating needs that are driving certain behaviors will equip you to diffuse most situations.

Organizations that acknowledge and properly manage the people part of change—whether that change emanates from the corner office down to the mailroom—are more likely to increase their odds for long-term success.

"Change is disturbing when it is done to us, exhilarating when it is done by us."
– Rosabeth Moss Kanter

The Role of Culture in Achieving Change

Your company culture reflects how and why things get done within your organization. It reflects employee behaviors, habits, and mindsets. Culture typically resists change because strong cultures are resistant and steadfast. Your culture is inevitably aligned with your business strategy and success. It is tried and true. Therefore, changing your culture is difficult. Here are three common mistakes to avoid regarding the role of culture in change.

- Failure to recognize the role culture plays in your change's success.
- An unwillingness among leaders to change their mindsets, behaviors, or styles.
- A disregard for the emotional side of culture change and the actions needed to address it.

However large or small your change is, the experience can feel uncomfortable for your employees. Change requires employees to break habits, go outside of their comfort zone, or adopt a practice they wouldn't necessarily engage in on their own. To effectively drive change, first understand that change won't happen overnight. It is a process that takes time.

How to Roll Out Changes at Your Company

Once you've uncovered the root of your business issues, getting the change management process right will help you get the results you want without as many headaches and frustrations.

Here are essential exercises to complete when rolling out changes at your company:

Set a goal and determine the best course of action to achieve it. Your goal is the "why" behind the change. Before determining what steps to take, make sure your leadership team is aligned on that "why." This will make it easier to figure out the best path forward.

You'll have plenty of ideas about how to take action, but narrow down your choices by asking yourself and your leadership team these questions:

- What top three strategies can we use to achieve our goal?
- Are those strategies feasible?
- What actions can we take *immediately* to get us where we need to be?

When you've answered those questions, you'll know what to do. Then, it's just a matter of how you're going to do it.

Figure out *how* you're going to take action and communicate it. Sometimes your action plan can fit right in with existing processes. Other times, you'll have to create new processes around it.

For example, if your change involves revamping company meeting habits, think about where you can positively change existing actions in order to achieve your desired results. When meetings are scheduled, ask employees to include agendas in calendar invitations. The action of sending out an invitation already exists; all you're doing is slightly tweaking behavior to make that action more impactful.

If your change requires a new process, it's best to roll that change out incrementally. If you want your meetings to be more efficient, consider first introducing a "time cop" to keep the meeting on track. Once that habit is adopted, you can create a process around opening with a verbal agenda and closing with next steps. The steps complement each other and will make the process second nature before you know it.

No matter how large or small the change, *effective communication* is essential. **Communicating early and often is the difference between success and failure in adoption**. Craft the best messaging possible so it resonates with everyone. Be transparent!

Some employees will prefer to learn about change through an all-company meeting or one-on-one conversations with their managers. Other employees may get more value out of an email. The more the message resonates and is delivered in a way that best suits your employees' communication styles, the more likely they will be to feel valued and invested in the change.

Ensure that you are allowing a two-way dialogue for questions to be asked and that you are encouraging and collecting feedback along the way.

Anticipate resistance and identify your champions. Your employees will naturally respond to change differently. Some may be excited, some will likely be indifferent, and others may be skeptical, uncomfortable, or even anxious. But you can easily anticipate resistance and identify the employees who will champion change.

You will always have *early adopters* to change and *naysayers*, with the majority of your people in the middle, unsure of the change. The mistake most people make is trying to convince *naysayers* to come on board to the change. That most likely won't happen in the near future, if at all. Have your *early adopters*, your champions, help drive the change and bring people on board, especially the majority in the middle. If your *naysayers* are poisoning the well for others or sabotaging the change and the culture, act quickly and remove them.

Use people data. There are two sets of people data essential to anticipating how employees will respond to change: an *employee experience survey* to measure engagement and *behavioral data* to measure your employees' drives and needs.

I had a client that went through a substantial office renovation —they added stairways to connect floors (versus elevators), converted walls and offices to glass, opened up spaces, and upgraded chairs and desks to be more ergonomic, including the addition of sit and stand desks, in addition to a number of other added benefits and features. It was a massive and expensive undertaking to improve employee connection, collaboration, energy, morale, and productivity. The CEO and COO were thrilled and excited to inform their hundreds of employees. What they did not expect was 30% of the employees reacting in disappointment and even threatening to leave.

They were surprised by the reaction and reached out to me in a bit of a panic. I asked them a number of questions, including whether they had sat down with employee representatives to discuss the plans and how they would impact the work environment. They hadn't. I reminded them of the talent analytics—in this case, we used PI—we had done for their entire workforce population, which provided tremendous insights on how their employees would react to risk and change, including how to involve them and communicate with them. About 30% of their employees would see any significant change as a threat. Involving them in advance so they would have a voice and input would have allowed them to contribute, influence, and understand the impact of the change in their ability to do their job well.

Hindsight is 20/20, but we developed a strategy to re-engage employees by soliciting input and feedback and discussing the impact of the change on their jobs.

Employee experience surveys will help you organize your employees into four groups:

Cultural Champions (high-performing, high engagement): These employees believe in your company values and work hard to reinforce them while also delivering tangible results. Involve them in the rollout process so they can evangelize the changes on the ground.

Grinders (high-performing, low engagement): These high achievers get the work done but feel removed from the company. Give them reasons to feel invested in your mission while also feeling you're invested *in them*. Once they're bought in, Grinders will turn into Cultural Champions.

Silent Killers (low-performing, high engagement): While they may love coming to work, Silent Killers don't always like *doing* their work. Anticipate some resistance here. If the change you're rolling out demands more output and higher-quality work, Silent Killers can quickly turn into Contaminators. On the flip side, if you communicate clear performance expectations, some Silent Killers may rise to the occasion and turn into Cultural Champions.

Contaminators (low-performing, low engagement): This is where you can expect the most resistance. Contaminators aren't delivering results, and they aren't invested in your company's mission. Change may turn these employees into flight risks, but this turnover may be best for both the company and your Contaminators. If they don't leave, I strongly recommend moving them out of your organization quickly before they poison your people, culture, and change effort. As the saying goes, if they don't want to get on the bus or stay on the bus, then it's time to get them off the bus.

Encourage your employees to become a part of the change management process in the way that best suits their natural strengths and abilities. Use behavioral data, like PI, to determine how they can best be involved.

For example, there will always be employees who are naturally more dominant and want to drive change. Leverage this drive by having those employees lead projects or key initiatives.

Complement your drivers by leveraging employees who are more stabilizing and can help keep projects on track, as well as those who are skilled at executing. Some employees will see change as a threat or risk and will need to understand how the change will impact their ability to still do their job. **Behavioral data and analytics will not only help you understand how to effectively manage change but will also help you understand how your managers will help manage change and what support they will need to be effective.**

You can't please everyone. But you can give your employees the opportunity to be change agents. When you're rolling out a change, remember to stay true to your purpose, your company mission, and your cultural values—it will make your company even stronger.

Not everyone will always be on board with change, and that's okay.

Don't resist change; embrace it! Stay true to who you are while being adaptive and agile. Remember, insanity is to continue to do the same things over and over again and expect different results!

Chapter 23: Talent Optimization

Take a good hard look at your company or organization. Is it performing at its absolute best? If you're like most leaders, you struggle to overcome common business challenges like turnover, employee disengagement, a changing market, bad hires—the list goes on and on. In spite of your best efforts *and* your best intentions, you can't quite accelerate your company's performance.

If you can relate to this everyday scenario, you likely struggle from a talent gap. This gap causes low productivity, poor results, and missed opportunities—it's the reason why most companies fail to perform at their highest potential.

If you're tired of falling short, talent optimization is the answer.

What Is Talent Optimization?

As a business leader, you're looking to drive results. You start each year with a strategy—what you're going to accomplish and how you're going to accomplish it. Yet 52% of CEOs surveyed by The Predictive Index's annual CEO Benchmarking Report said they didn't achieve their business results last year. Why is that? Regardless of what kind of organization you're in, your results are driven by people. And if your people aren't aligned with your strategy ... well, let's just say that's where that 52% comes in.

It's your job as a business leader to make sure your company optimizes its talent so you can achieve your objectives and crush the competition. The best way to do this is talent optimization— exactly what you're about to get a crash course in.

Talent optimization uses data and analytics to help you define job requirements, identify ideal candidates for open positions, align teams to accomplish business goals, and effectively inspire employees for optimal results.

This discipline is founded on four essential truths:

- Talent optimization exists within a business context.
- Talent optimization is driven by "people" data.
- Talent optimization must be embraced by leaders at every level.
- Talent optimization protects against the four forces of disengagement.

Let's explore the essential truths of talent optimization.

Essential Truth #1: Talent optimization exists within a business context.

Talent optimization doesn't happen in a vacuum—it's informed by business strategy and exists within a business context.

Your business strategy is at the heart of your talent optimization efforts. It informs your people strategy and is the meter you'll measure your actions and decisions against.

Talent optimization isn't about changing your business strategy; it's a way of taking your organization's thoughtful, well-designed strategy and using it to guide the way you hire people, build teams, and design your culture, among other actions.

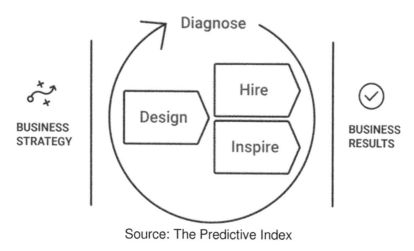

Source: The Predictive Index

For talent optimization to work, the business strategy must meet five criteria. The strategy must be:

Deliberate. It should be written following careful consideration of how your company competes, prospers, delivers on its mission, leverages external opportunities and internal assets, and structures its operations.

Simple. It should have a narrow focus. A strategy that aims to do too many things will fail.

Actionable. It should be worded in a way that allows the leadership team to prepare a plan for execution. Example: "Competing on the basis of innovation."

Agreed upon. It should be agreed upon by all key stakeholders. Every stakeholder must be aligned on what the strategy is and how it should be executed.

Communicated. It should be communicated so all employees understand the goals the company is trying to achieve.

Essential Truth #2: Talent optimization is driven by "people" data.

When it comes to executing a talent strategy, "people" data empowers business leaders to make objective decisions, rather than relying on gut feeling. There are a number of tools and techniques leaders can leverage to collect and measure this data, such as PI, employee engagement surveys, climate surveys, etc.

While no one tool can accurately tell you everything about an individual, that doesn't mean you can't leverage data to predict performance. In fact, when using the right tools, like PI, it's possible to predict how people will behave and interact in organizations. These insights help talent optimizers understand the people in their organization and make improvements to the way they work.

Essential Truth #3: Talent optimization must be embraced by leaders at every level.

If talent optimization isn't adopted by leaders at every level of your organization, it won't work.

Organizations that implement talent optimization must adopt the mantra of "leaders at every level." This mindset considers everyone—from senior leadership to frontline managers to individual contributors—to be a leader.

Essential Truth #4: Talent optimization protects against the four forces of disengagement.

Recently, The Predictive Index (MCG Partners is a licensed partner firm of The Predictive Index) surveyed 3,000 people and found that only 20% of employees identify as strongly engaged at work. *This means only one out of every five employees would say they're proud to work for their organization, would recommend their company as a great place to work, are happy working at their organization, and would have to be convinced very strongly to leave.* That also means that 80% of your workforce wouldn't strongly agree with one of those four statements.

We define engagement as putting in "discretionary effort" and going above and beyond the minimum requirements to keep one's job and receive a paycheck. When this discretionary effort is missing, business results suffer—whether as a result of poor productivity, absenteeism, safety issues, poor client service, or a toxic workplace culture.

Master the Key to Driving Business Results.

Diagnose: Measure what matters. Talent optimization reminds us that all talent activities take place within the business context. For this reason, it's important to collect the right people data *and* business data when operating in an agile organization. The behavioral profiles of team members are a critical type of people data for the Agile Leader. This type of data fosters self-awareness and awareness of others' behavioral similarities and differences. This can help the business leaders understand team members who are naturally well-suited for an agile approach, and those for whom it may be a stretch.

Agile methodologies also lend themselves well to data collection and tracking key metrics. Some examples of agile data points include measures of on-time delivery, productivity, and customer satisfaction. It's important to use these objective measures as context for the people-dependent aspects of proper agile execution.

Design: Select your organization's structure. An agile strategy demands flexibility, adaptation, and efficient collaboration. These success factors immediately tell us something about the required organizational structure. A hierarchical, top-down model has many strengths, but supporting an agile methodology is not one of them. Too many tiers of management and approval will stifle communication and speedy decision-making.

By contrast, a flat or network structure — one that allows for self-organizing "teams of teams" — is more common in the world of agile. In this type of structure, information flows quickly and easily. Leadership is diffused throughout an autonomous team that's guided by a shared sense of purpose and a clear goal. Continuous experimentation and learning are hallmarks of this type of organizational structure.

Hire: Determine candidate cultural fit. An agile organization requires innovation, collaboration, entrepreneurship, and a performance orientation. It's important to integrate these values deeply into the organization's culture. When evaluating candidates for hire or promotion, it's therefore important to consider the individual's cultural fit across these same dimensions. Can the candidate demonstrate specific examples when they embodied one or more of these values in their work? When they ask questions about the opportunity, are these values involved? Also consider someone who can bring something new, where they can add to and improve the culture while still fitting the culture.

Inspire: Create high-performing teams. Team dynamics are important to the successful execution of any business strategy, but an agile methodology places a premium on team communication, decision-making, and taking action. Communication in an agile organization is fast and furious. The teams must all strive to keep one another up to date on their respective purpose, goals, progress, and changes made in a dynamic environment. Agile organizations require swift action and response, so decision-making must also be expedited. Finally, it's important for an agile organization to have a bias for taking action. Boldness is always favorable in the pursuit of innovation and an entrepreneurial approach.

Organizations that adopt agile structures and methodologies aim to increase innovation, customer satisfaction, and operating efficiency, as well as see a general increase in competitiveness and performance. Leaders who are able to adopt the mindset and behaviors required to execute this shift are well-positioned to create greater value for their organizations, their customers, and themselves. For this reason, the talent optimization discipline and framework can be an important guide for leaders in an agile transformation.

There Are Four Key Causes of Disengagement

As mentioned in chapter 18, there are four key causes of disengagement. They are:

Misalignment with the job: When positions are poorly defined, hiring isn't thoughtful, or organizational growth changes the job description, it can create misalignment between the employee and their role.

Misalignment with the manager: Managers play a crucial role in employee engagement, yet many managers lack the knowledge or training to successfully motivate and manage their employees.

Misalignment with the team: More and more, teamwork is required to execute strategy. However, poor communication and discord between varying personalities take a toll on productivity and innovation.

Misalignment with culture: Employees need to feel like they belong to something bigger than themselves. When they feel misaligned with the organization's values or distrustful of its leadership, engagement takes a nosedive.

Now that we've got the four essential truths down, let's look at the four aptitudes of the talent optimization discipline.

Aptitude #1: Diagnose

In this aptitude, you'll take the pulse of your organization. In the same way a doctor runs tests to formally diagnose a patient, you'll collect and measure critical people data, analyze that data in the context of your business, and prescribe solutions.

The Diagnose aptitude is made up of three activities:

Put measurements in place. Most businesses track and measure key performance indicators for sales, customer satisfaction, and the like. Here, you'll take a similar approach in measuring important people data such as behavioral styles, culture, employee engagement, and job performance.

Analyze the evidence. With your people data in hand, it's time to analyze the evidence within your business context. This will provide insights into issues that may not be obvious on the surface so you can quickly and effectively take action. Follow up with employees to get clarity on findings so you can pinpoint the key drivers of disengagement and prioritize your action plans.

Prescribe improvement actions. This is where you'll create a tactical plan of action to correct the issues you discovered when analyzing your people data. The goal is to make important changes that will help the organization achieve its desired business results.

Aptitude #2: Design

In this aptitude, you'll create a people strategy that's in alignment with your business strategy. Keep in mind that your people strategy will continually evolve as the needs of your organization change.

The Design aptitude is made up of four activities:

Select your organization's structure. Your organizational structure should be intentional, strategic, and aligned with the business results you're looking to achieve.

Evaluate your leadership team fit. Here you'll assess the leadership abilities required to execute on your business strategy, so you can identify any gaps within your existing senior leadership team and make plans to address them.

Understand senior team dynamics. A cohesive senior leadership team is a critical component of talent optimization. Developing awareness of personal and collective strengths—as well as similarities and differences—will encourage productivity.

Establish your culture. Culture needs to be deliberately and intentionally constructed in alignment with the business strategy and communicated as such. This plays a crucial role in employee engagement and performance.

Aptitude #3: Hire

In this aptitude, you'll leverage the insights gained from collecting people data to hire top talent and build cohesive teams.

The Hire aptitude is made up of four activities:

Define and communicate job requirements. Job requirements go beyond the practical to include behavioral drives and cognitive ability needed to succeed in the role. Putting in the extra time and effort up front will allow you to quickly identify and hire candidates who are likely to be a great fit.

Equip your leaders to land top talent. Hiring can't be left to chance or gut feel. Training and equipping your hiring managers to use people data in the hiring process will enable them to make smart and objective hiring decisions.

Predict new team dynamics. Healthy team dynamics are critical to accomplishing strategic goals. Using people data to evaluate team fit prior to making the hire increases chances of success.

Determine candidate cultural fit. Creating and maintaining company culture is a key component of talent optimization. When evaluating job candidates, consider their potential impact on and alignment with your organizational culture.

Aptitude #4: Inspire

In this aptitude, you'll take the data gained from the *Diagnose* aptitude to drive important employee engagement initiatives. This includes career pathing, building and maintaining a healthy company culture, and managing people and teams.

The Inspire aptitude is made up of four activities:

Create new jobs and career paths. Over time, you'll need to create new jobs and career paths, and modify job roles to stay aligned with your business strategy. Anticipating these needs allows you to hire the right talent and keep current talent growing and engaged.

Develop your leaders. Leadership competencies are one of the top drivers of employee engagement. By identifying and evaluating leadership abilities, and giving performance feedback within a business context, you set the stage for high engagement and performance.

Build high-performing teams. All teams should aim to become high-performing so the organization can achieve its goals. Senior leadership must set the tone for the rest of the organization when it comes to decision-making, collaboration, and taking action.

Reinforce your culture. Culture can't be left to chance. An unmonitored and unmanaged culture will quickly become toxic, zapping engagement, and productivity.

Educate yourself on how to align your employees with your business strategy and arm yourself with talent optimization tools that provide you with people data insights. This way you can take a data-driven approach to hiring the right people, designing your culture, diagnosing engagement levels, and managing employees effectively.

Want to close the talent gap once and for all? With talent optimization, you finally can.

Talent Optimization Practices That Drive Superior Business Results

While having an agreed upon and well-documented business strategy is mission critical, business strategies don't execute themselves; people do. Senior leaders can maximize strategic performance by crafting an aligned talent strategy that mobilizes employees to handle the execution themselves.

The PI recently surveyed 600 executives, including 200 CEOs, across 20 industries to understand the relationship between talent optimization and company performance. The survey found a relationship between talent optimization and company performance. In fact, the results showed that specific combinations of talent optimization practices translated into positive business results.

A key finding of the study found that **talent optimized companies outperform other companies by 16%** in terms of strategic success rates.

When companies implemented the following talent optimization practices, their strategic success rate increased to almost 90%.

- Align talent strategy to the business strategy.
- Align organizational structure to the business strategy.
- Ensure talent strategy is well-documented and understood throughout the organization.
- Make talent strategy everyone's responsibility (not just HR's).
- Have the right executive team in place to execute the business strategy.
- Understand executives' confidence level in achieving each strategic priority.

Considering that even high-velocity companies may only be able to pursue a few strategic initiatives each year—each being a substantial investment of time and resources—improving those strategic outcomes' success rate by 16% is an enormous differentiator in the market.

Conclusion

"You cannot get through a single day without having an impact on the world around you. What you do makes a difference, and you have to decide what kind of difference you want to make." – Jane Goodall

The biggest impact of losing my father, so suddenly, at a young age, was the realization that our time can be up in a heartbeat. We don't know when it will be our time to go. There's nothing we can do about it, and we shouldn't dwell on it or stress about it. However, you can live in the present and enjoy each moment. You can ask yourself an important question each and every day: are you doing the best you can for yourself and others? If your life were to end in the next few minutes, would you be content that you lived the life you wanted to live and made a difference, even to just one person?

The Self-Fulfilling Prophecy

Self-fulfilled prophecies occur when your self-imposed expectations influence your behavior. A *self-fulfilling prophecy* is a belief that comes true because we are acting as if it is already true.

There are two sides of the self-fulfilling prophecy: on one side, you are concerned, stressed, and maybe even obsessed with what could go wrong, or if you are good enough, or if you belong. If you focus too much on these types of thoughts, you will fulfill them. The opposite is also true: if you believe and see yourself reaching certain heights or if you see yourself building an amazing team and organization, and overcoming obstacles, and improving yourself - you can fulfill those visions.

Pay attention to both sides of the self-fulfilling prophecy, as they will come true if you believe it.

The Power of One

One person can make a difference.

The Five P's.

With purpose and passion, you can make progress, impact people, and deliver performance.

Do not underestimate yourself and others' character, resilience, capability, and desire to make a difference.

Don't wait. Don't wait for someone else.

Time is precious. Start now. Start today.

Lead the way.

Articulate and demonstrate a vision, engage others who are inspired, and share that vision. Create champions of that vision to begin to make changes every day for your aspirational destination.

It takes a village. Surround yourself with good people in all aspects of your life. One plus one equals three. *Recognize the power of many with a united purpose.*

Contribute to the greater good. Find your voice and a vision. Others will follow, and surprising things can happen—even cultural changes on a large scale. Your voice can spark the voices of many others, offering a path and vision for a more positive future for all.

Becoming an Agile Leader *is* the future of leadership.

As leaders of today and tomorrow, we need to balance our internal and external focus. We need to empower teams and organizations to be agile: decisive, nimble, empowering, and experimental. We are in a new era of business, of connections, of information management, and of understanding of what people value.

We need to embrace everyone's differences, experiences, and views.

Leaders need to understand the lens of others to appreciate how they see and think. We need to expand our capacity for healthy relationships and how we create a safe work environment and accept mistakes and failures to innovate. It's all about trust—trusting ourselves and others, through improved self-awareness and enriched insights of others.

Becoming an Agile Leader matters. It matters for you, your team, and your organization, to rapidly respond to the constant and increasing changes around us.

I look back with amazement at the last 20 years, to when my leadership journey had a significant disruption: my first 360-degree assessment. It's been quite a road, a passage for me, one that I'm still on. From my childhood to high school and college years, and throughout my professional and personal life and experiences, I've learned to appreciate many things. I have learned about pushing myself beyond what I thought I was capable of, never quitting on my dreams and aspirations to find my passion and purpose in life. I have experienced the value of deeply learning about myself, my blind spots, how I'm perceived by others, and accepting myself and others for who they are. I can adapt and learn new behaviors and skills to be effective with my relationships and how I influence and work with others without compromising my values, beliefs, and authenticity. I understand the importance of shifting from *me* to *them* to *you*.

I've worked with leaders and executives from around the world, in every industry, type, and size of company. I've been inspired by many who have transformed in front of my eyes and their people's eyes. It's been such an honor to have participated and collaborated in their experiences and change.

The principles I've covered in this book transformed me, helped me understand myself and others—and that's why I wanted to share them with you. These techniques will help you on your path, your journey of what successful leadership is for you. If you follow them, you will find what it means to develop others and have a positive impact on the world around you.

Create that meaningful culture. Start with your direct team, and then expand to other teams and the enterprise.

What now?

What will be the things you will begin to work on today? Will you be doing things differently? How will you be applying your new learning, knowledge, techniques, and approaches to becoming a better version of yourself?

How will you make a shift to become an Agile Leader?

I applaud your curiosity, and your interest to question and challenge yourself, and the world around you. Be a truth seeker and help make the world a better place. Ask for input and feedback because people want to help if you let them. Start with yourself, and then one person, one team, one organization, and one community at a time.

If, in reading this book, you have been inspired and motivated to do things differently, to take on a new path, to become more self-aware, and to rededicate or dedicate yourself to the quest of leadership, please reach out to me. Let me know how you are doing. You can reach me at chuck.mollor@mcgpartners.com.

I wish you to be your best.
Chuck Mollor

About the Author

Chuck Mollor is the founder, CEO, and executive coach at MCG Partners and author of the book, *The Rise of The Agile Leader: Can You Make the Shift?* MCG Partners specializes in leadership and talent optimization, aligning business and people strategy for maximum results.

For over 30 years Chuck has advised, coached, and consulted executives and organizations across industries, from startups to Fortune 500 and not-for-profit organizations. As an executive coach and strategic advisor, Chuck determines if an organization's leadership and culture are aligned to its business strategy, then develops and implements solutions to drive and attain results.

Chuck develops current and potential leaders and C-level executives, aligns, and optimizes leadership teams, and helps create a leadership culture reflective of the organization's purpose and vision.

As a former Harvard Business School executive coach, Chuck provided, and continues to provide, coaching and advisory services to global executives. He is also a member of the Forbes Coaches Council, an invitation-only council for leading executive coaches.

In his former roles as a global CEO and member of several executive teams, Chuck has a breadth of experience with general management and P&L responsibilities, and ran, built, started, and restructured several businesses. Chuck has led strategy, sales, marketing, product development, operations, HR, and a global partnership of more than 100 consulting firms.

Chuck is a graduate of executive programs at The Harvard Business School, MIT Sloan School of Management, and The Wharton School of the University of Pennsylvania. He has a BA in political science and a minor in business administration from Merrimack College and is a PI certified Talent Optimization Consultant and in The Predictive Index Behavioral Assessment™.

Chuck serves on several boards of directors, is a Cranberry Grower-Owner of Ocean Spray, and a fundraiser and rider for the Pan-Mass Challenge (PMC), a 192-mile bike ride for the fight against cancer. Chuck lives near Boston, Massachusetts with his wife, four children, and two dogs.

Made in United States
North Haven, CT
21 March 2022

17406806R00157